IMAGES
of America

OCCIDENTAL

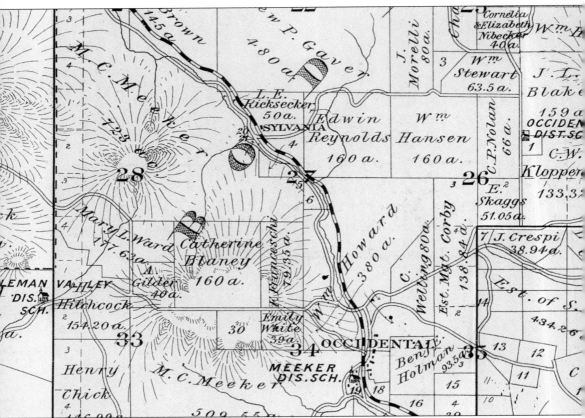

OCCIDENTAL, 1898. This map is from an 1898 Reynolds and Proctor atlas showing the early town of Occidental. The image shows the Occidental, Coleman Valley, and Meeker School Districts and many of the landowners who helped shape the town. Landowners shown on the map include Meeker, Howard, Coleman, Proctor, Taylor, Hansen, Glynn, Bones, and Franceschi. (Courtesy Library of Congress.)

ON THE COVER: OCCIDENTAL, 1903. This photograph shows the Good Friends Saloon, sometimes referred by the local Italians as the "Goodie Friends" Saloon. Members of the Pozzi, Donati, Franceschi, Gonnella, Guidici, Morelli, and Paladini families are gathered in front of the saloon. Achille Paladini stands on the far right in front of his shoemaker's shop. (Courtesy Frank and Barbara Gonnella family.)

IMAGES
of America

OCCIDENTAL

Barbara Gonnella, Mary Pozzi,
and Bob Dougherty

ARCADIA
PUBLISHING

Published by Arcadia Publishing
Charleston, South Carolina

Printed in the United States of America

Library of Congress Control Number: 2019949049

For all general information, please contact Arcadia Publishing:
Telephone 843-853-2070
Fax 843-853-0044
E-mail sales@arcadiapublishing.com
For customer service and orders:
Toll-Free 1-888-313-2665

Visit us on the Internet at www.arcadiapublishing.com

OCCIDENTAL, C. 1905. Since the inception of Occidental in 1876, the town has been affected by many catastrophic events, including family tragedies, the Great San Francisco Earthquake of 1906, and the fires of 1899, 1906, and 1924. But after each of these events, the town has always united to rebuild and strengthen its community. This photograph shows the town in about 1905, highlighted by the steeple of the Methodist Episcopal Church, the oldest building in Occidental. (Courtesy Harold Lapham.)

CONTENTS

ACKNOWLEDGMENTS

The authors would like to thank the following historians, local families, and other contributors for helping make this book possible: Harold Lapham, Gaye LeBaron, Eleanor Travaglini, Beverly Stumbaugh, Bob and Lavon Sturgeon, Jay Meyer, St. Dorothy's Rest, Westminster Woods, Alliance Redwoods, Catholic Charities Catholic Youth Organization Camp, Eric Koenigshofer, Nick Gravenites, Mickey and Caryl Hart, Gienna Michel Gonnella, Frank Gonnella, Lucille Gonnella, Caren Normandin, the John Calvi family, Harvey Henningsen, Sylvia Fisher, Dennis Morelli, George Fiori, Evelyn Negri, Sandy Negri, Amanda Negri, Bob Panizzera, June Rossini, Barbara Rossini, Aliza Wheeler, Jessica Wheeler, Tami Fiori Mesenbrink, Nancy Facendini, Joe Lunardi, Linda Marra, Dawna Mirante, Sonoma County History and Genealogy Library, Judith Draft, L.W. Proctor Collection, Teres Pozzi Santos, Jude Pozzi Mercieca, Eileen Pozzi Jensen, Yvonne Thompson, Jocelyn Gardner, the Priest family, John Gonnella, Jack Journey, Occidental Volunteer Fire Department, Cathie Lunardi, Dan Pozzi, Maribell Pozzi, Greg Browder, Kevin Illia, Karen Redmond Webber, Walt Fitzpatrick Ryan, Patty Maloney Blake, Jim Maloney, Susan Brunson, Brook O' Conner, Nancy Kelly Wheeler, Annie Neustadter Harvey, Julie Neustadter, Bob Maddocks, Elizabeth Morelli Perry, Brad Respini, Rick Garcia, and Carolyn Douglas.

INTRODUCTION

Occidental is a small, unincorporated town in Sonoma County, California, about 60 miles north of San Francisco and 10 miles east of the Pacific Ocean. The town is located on a saddle that divides two watersheds—the Salmon Creek watershed and Dutch Bill Creek watershed. This book will cover both the town of Occidental and some of the surrounding unincorporated areas nearby bounded by Monte Rio to the northwest and Freestone to the southeast. It will not cover the community of Camp Meeker north of Occidental, which is deserving of a separate account of its own rich history. Like ancient Rome, all nearby roads seem to lead to the town of Occidental—Graton Road, Occidental Road, Coleman Valley Road, Bittner Road, and the Bohemian Highway running through the center of town.

Occidental has cool, wet winters and warm, dry summers. The town's elevation is 594 feet, which is high enough to prevent the flooding that commonly occurs in other areas near the Russian River. The population of Occidental was 1,115 in the 2010 census, but this number belies the many thousands of visitors each year who come to enjoy the natural beauty or dine in its famous Italian restaurants.

Until 1876, the town had no definitive name. The first railroad men called it Summit because Occidental was the highest point on the railroad. Others called it Howards, after William "Dutch Bill" Howard, who owned most of the town and required that the train depot be named after him in exchange for right-of-way access. Lumber baron Melvin Cyrus Meeker in his 1880 biography claimed that he was the one who named it Occidental. Although Meeker may have popularized the name, the nearby Occidental School District existed in 1864 before Meeker lived in the area, so there was already a precedent for the name. The reason for the school district being called Occidental, which can just mean western, may have been because it was located in the western part of Sonoma County. Perhaps a rivalry between Meeker and Howard compelled Meeker to call the town anything other than Howards, and trying to call the town Meeker at the time may have appeared egotistical. But Meeker would soon have a community named after him, Camp Meeker, a mile north of Occidental. Although letters from the time reveal that the old-timers continued to use the names Summit and Howards, the town seemed destined to accept the name Occidental after the post office used the name in 1876. An early newspaper reference to the name was on December 29, 1876, in a letter to the *Petaluma Weekly Argus* saying that, with the businesses, railroad, and now post office there, "Occidental may now be considered a town."

This book will cover Occidental from its earliest beginnings to the current day, although the concentration will be on its first 50 years, approximately 1875 to 1925. These were the formative years of the town, and the current town is still greatly influenced by the early settlers and events of this era. Occidental during these years drew opportunists from many countries searching for a better life. Opportunities for many of them did occur, but their workdays were often long and difficult. By necessity, these early settlers acquired diverse skills as the seasons and times changed, including farming, dairying, and logging. The arrival of the railroad in 1876 allowed lumber, charcoal, dairy, and agricultural products to be quickly transported to San Francisco, and in return, goods from San Francisco were transported back to Occidental. Along with these goods came visitors, including campers and other recreationists, often vacationing in what they considered wilderness. By the 1920s, a large number of Italians had settled in the area and opened competing restaurants. By 1930, most of the commercial lumber industry had ended because of wildfires and unsustainable tree harvesting, and the Great Depression paralyzed the country for the next decade. The year 1930 was also when the last passenger and freight trains left Occidental; America had already begun her love affair with the automobile.

Generations of families continued to return to Occidental to experience the authentic Italian cuisine; however, Occidental still remained relatively isolated until the 1960s and 1970s. At that time, young newcomers arrived with ideas and values vastly different than the older immigrants. They saw in these newcomers a decrease in morality, an increase in illicit drug use, and a seeming disdain for hard work. These counterculturists protested for peace during the Vietnam War, supported equality and civil rights, experimented with mind-altering drugs, and had a more carefree attitude toward sex and nudity. Sometimes they visited or moved into nearby communes, such as Morningstar or Wheeler ranch. These newcomers were the bane of some of the older residents who saw the stability of their traditional lifestyle and community fractured. There was a resulting culture clash and disagreement on many issues between older, more traditional farmers and immigrants with the younger hippies and artists. Eventually, however, both sides joined forces to ensure that Occidental maintained its character and charm in the longer term.

This book is an abbreviated history of Occidental and the surrounding area, mainly told through available photographs. Although the authors have tried to highlight the most important pioneers and families in Occidental, we have likely missed some because of the brevity of this book. In addition, we have tried to be accurate in the names, dates, and events, but some of the information has come from fallible memories, single sources, or conflicting accounts. If you do find something that you believe is not accurate, please send an e-mail to occidentalhistory@lahonda.com so it can be corrected in a future edition of this book.

One

EARLY AND NATURAL HISTORY

The Occidental area consists primarily of two geologic formations: the Franciscan-Knoxville and the Merced formations. The Franciscan-Knoxville formation is sandstone and siltstone from the Upper Jurassic age, whereas the Merced formation is much more recent. The landscape is still forming, as several miles away along the coast is the active San Andreas Fault. Movement from this fault caused substantial damage in Occidental in the 1906 earthquake. The abundance of rainfall and a temperate climate in this evolving landscape create an environment conducive and attractive to a large number of plants and animals.

The Pomo are an indigenous people who arrived between 8,000 and 5,000 BCE and lived in small groups in the area. These groups were linked by location, language, and culture. The Pomo fished, hunted, and gathered food. Their diet included salmon, mushrooms, berries, rabbits, rats, squirrels, and especially, acorns. They were also known for their intricate basketry. In 1800, there were estimated to be between 10,000 and 18,000 Pomo, but the early European migrants brought infectious diseases like smallpox and measles, and by 1880, the Pomo population was estimated to be only 1,450. Many Pomo groups are now designated by the United States as federally recognized tribes, which allows them to live with some autonomy from the US and California governments.

The European settlers logged most of the old-growth redwoods for lumber, stripped the tanbark oaks for leather tannins, and fished and hunted in ways that were unsustainable. Many fires accidentally set by the settlers turned into massive wildfires, and these early settlers had no effective way to fight the blazes. In 1899, 1906, and 1924, fires destroyed much of the town of Occidental and surrounding areas. By 1925, environmental destruction was widespread from logging and fires, but awareness and attitudes have since changed, and the forests are now healing.

WATERSHED. Watersheds catch and store rainwater based on climate, elevation, soil, plants, and slope. A watershed then drains into a distinct creek or river. Occidental is unusual in that it is located on a saddle that divides the town between two watersheds—Salmon Creek and Dutch Bill Creek watersheds. Redwood-covered hills surround the town, as shown in this 1902 photograph. These features help create an idyllic setting for the town. (Courtesy Harold Lapham.)

AREA GEOLOGY. The Occidental area primarily consists of two geologic formations: the Franciscan-Knoxville and the Merced formations. Part of the Camp Meeker serpentine sill, shown here, is a distinct feature of the greater area. Serpentine, the state rock of California, is exposed as treeless outcroppings for over six miles. Likely started as a rumor to attract investors, the *Sonoma West Times and News* in 1898 said, "A quantity of gold-bearing rock was found on Stephen Meeker's ranch near Occidental." (Courtesy Dawna Mirante.)

FLOODS AND DROUGHTS. Occidental is located at an elevation of 594 feet with an average annual rainfall of about 55 inches. Because of this elevation, the town is not as vulnerable to flooding as much of the nearby Russian River area. However, flooding, downed trees, and mudslides can isolate the town in winter. Like much of California, Occidental also experiences periodic droughts. This photograph shows a swollen Dutch Bill Creek after winter rains. (Courtesy Barbara Gonnella.)

FIRE, 1924. Occidental suffered a number of devastating fires. One began on New Year's Eve in 1899 and burned down much of the town, including the W.B. Coy General Merchandise Store, the post office, Montreal Saloon, Odd Fellow's Hall, and the butcher's shop. A 1924 blaze also destroyed most of the town, including the Gonnella Store, Brians's Garage, Panizzera Butcher Shop, Fehr Jewelry, Altamont Hotel, and the Community Store. This photograph is looking east through town after the 1924 fire. (Courtesy Sonoma County Library.)

EARTHQUAKE, W.B. COY GENERAL MERCHANDISE STORE, 1906. A major earthquake hazard in the area is the San Andreas Fault, which extends in a north-south direction just west of Bodega Head. The April 18, 1906, earthquake damaged much of the town and the nearby railroad tracks. This photograph shows repair work on the Coy store after the earthquake. The Coy store was well stocked at the time, supplying everything from underwear to undertaking supplies. (Courtesy Sonoma County Library.)

EARTHQUAKE, HANSEN BUILDING, 1906. The Hansen Building survived a major fire in March 1906, only to be the one building in town destroyed by the April 1906 earthquake—primarily because it was constructed with unreinforced bricks. Of that day, Occidental resident Wade Sturgeon recalled that he was thrown out of bed, fell down the stairs, and saw a fire in the direction of San Francisco that "resembled a volcano it was so large." Pictured here are Mary McCandless and Jacob Fehr examining the destruction. (Courtesy Frank and Barbara Gonnella family.)

COASTAL REDWOODS, C. 1880. *Sequoia sempervirens* are the tallest trees on earth, can grow over 350 feet, and can live 1,800 years or more. Moisture from coastal fog can provide much of the trees' water needs. Commercial logging of redwoods near Occidental started in the 1860s, driven by mining and building timber needs triggered by the California Gold Rush. Opposition to the extensive logging was slow and largely ineffective, and it took decades to protect what little remains of old-growth redwoods. (Courtesy the Bob Sturgeon family.)

OAK WOODLAND, C. 1960. The area near Occidental supports a variety of species of oaks, including the tanbark oak or tanoak (*Notholithocarpus densiflorus*). Oak wood is used for furniture, flooring, whiskey and wine barrels, and firewood. The bark of tanoak was used for tanning leather, although synthetic tannins are used today. Many of these oaks have been affected by the often fatal "sudden oak death" pathogen. (Courtesy Sonoma County Library.)

ENDANGERED ANIMALS. Extensive logging and other human activity have caused many species to become extinct, endangered, or threatened. Threatened animals include the Coho salmon, steelhead trout, northern spotted owl, California red-legged frog, and the California tiger salamander. Recovery plans are underway for these creatures, but their habitats may be too damaged for some of them to ever recover. The threatened northern spotted owl, shown here, lives in old-growth forests. (Courtesy US National Park Service.)

MAMMALS. There are many mammals in the Occidental area, including various species of squirrels, foxes, bobcats, coyotes, raccoons, skunks, mountain lions, weasels, mice, rats, bats, and deer. Black-tailed deer (*Odocoileus hemionus columbianus*), pictured, are sometimes referred to as the "Pacific ghost" because of their ability to move unheard and unseen. They are a subspecies of the mule deer, and their color can change from reddish-brown in summer to brownish-gray in winter. (Courtesy Brook O'Connor.)

SNOW, 1941. Snowstorms occasionally blanket Occidental. This photograph shows snow in 1941; there were also snowstorms in 1883, 1932, and 1974. However, Occidental usually has cool, wet winters and warm, dry summers. Average January temperatures range from about 42 to 55 degrees, and July temperatures range from 51 to 78 degrees. St. Philip the Apostle Catholic Church is seen here at right. (Courtesy Elizabeth Mazzotti.)

POMO GATHERING SEEDS, 1924. The indigenous inhabitants of the Occidental area were the Southern Pomo. The Pomo hunted and fished, and they gathered mushrooms, berries, and other foodstuffs. Acorns were a staple of their diet. The Pomo lived in the area for over 10,000 years before the first Spaniards and other European settlers arrived. Pictured is a Coast Pomo woman using a seed beater to gather seeds into a burden basket. (Courtesy Library of Congress.)

POMO ARTIFACTS. The Pomo had no written language, and their oral language became endangered after European colonization. They had elaborate acting and dancing ceremonies, created beautiful abalone and clamshell jewelry, and wove watertight baskets. Some Pomo incorporated feathers into the basket weave, so many baskets are both functional and works of art. Numerous durable Pomo artifacts, like the arrowheads seen here, have been found in the area. (Courtesy Bob Dougherty.)

POMO GIRL DURING GRAPE HARVEST, 1937. A young Pomo girl who worked with her mother during the harvest picking grapes, hops, and other agricultural products is seen here. European migrants brought infectious diseases like measles and smallpox into the area, which had high fatality rates among the Pomo, who had no natural immunity. The Pomo are designated by the United States as part of a federally recognized tribe. (Courtesy US Department of the Interior.)

Two

LIVES OF EARLY PIONEERS

Although the earliest human settlers near Occidental were the indigenous Pomo, countries like Spain, England, Russia, and Mexico each claimed the area starting in the 16th century. Fort Ross near the coast was established by Russians looking for timber, fur, and land for farming in 1812. Farther east, the Spanish founded their last, northernmost mission in 1821.

The early pioneers to the Occidental area were primarily driven by opportunity—some for the gold rush and others because of the abundance of arable land. Europe, and even the East Coast of the United States, was getting relatively crowded, and farm and ranch land was unavailable or unusable. Once these early pioneers arrived, many discovered other opportunities in businesses because of the rapidly expanding economy. In 1879, there were 5,774 registered voters in Sonoma County with about 1,500 of them naturalized foreigners. They were led by Ireland, then Germany, England, Scotland, France, and Italy.

One of the earliest known European settlers near Occidental was Patrick McCue, a native of Ireland who lived alone; unfortunately, little else is known about him. Another early family was that of Michael and Josefa Kolmer, who Coleman Valley was named after. Their daughter Caroline married William Howard, another early settler in the area. William "Dutch Bill" Howard was the assumed name of a Danish man who jumped ship in 1849 searching for gold and who wanted to conceal his identity.

Soon, other settlers, including Blaney, Connolly, Franceschi, and Gobetti, arrived by ship or overland. The population of Occidental in 1877 was estimated at 50, and in 1880, it was 97. Some of this population was native-born, but others were immigrants from Ireland, England, Denmark, Canada, and China. Soon afterward, between the 1880s and 1920s, the town had a heavy influx of Italian immigrants, especially from the Lombardy and Tuscany regions.

The early settlers had to be healthy and industrious to thrive in an isolated area like Occidental. Now rare because of vaccines, infectious diseases like measles, mumps, rubella, diphtheria, pertussis, polio, and hepatitis could cause epidemics and decimate families and communities. These stoic settlers accepted their hardships and relied on hard work and God to get through each day, and often alcohol to get through the evenings.

THE KOLMERS, C. 1855. Michael and Josepha Kolmer were perhaps the first settlers in the Occidental area, arriving with their three children in 1847. Their youngest daughter, Caroline, impulsively married William "Dutch Bill" Howard in 1855. Her father flew into a rage upon hearing the news, throwing all of Caroline's furniture and clothes into a bonfire. He then rounded up his friends, grabbed guns, and chased the newlyweds on horse. Michael Kolmer vowed never to see or speak to Caroline again; however, he later relented. (Courtesy Judith Daft.)

WILLIAM "DUTCH BILL" HOWARD, 1880. Dutch Bill Howard was a Danish sailor named Christopher Folkmann born in 1823. He was a seaman on the USS *St. Mary*, but deserted in 1849 after hearing about the gold in California. He stole a boat and headed north, ending up in what would become Occidental. Much of the town was later owned by Howard and M.C. Meeker. After Howard's wife died, heavy drinking and careless spending led to his financial ruin. (Courtesy Frank and Barbara Gonnella family.)

MORE EARLY SETTLERS. Some of the earliest settlers migrated across preindustrial America in covered wagons. Oxen were commonly used for pulling the wagons. The side of this wagon has several phrases, including "The Lord Be Blessed—We's Here." This 1904 photograph shows early settlers Jenny Beedle, Louis Beedle, John Blaney, Annie Rodgers, and Ben Brians. (Courtesy Sonoma County Library.)

MEEKER FAMILY, C. 1880. Meeker was perhaps the most important family in early Occidental, with Melvin Cyrus (M.C.) Meeker being thought of as the "founder of Occidental." He was instrumental in building the town at its present location. From left to right are (first row) sons Melvin Jr. and Alexander "Bert" II; (second row) daughter Effie, father Melvin Sr., wife Flavia, and son Robert. (Courtesy Frank and Barbara Gonnella family.)

MELVIN CYRUS "BOSS" MEEKER, C. 1920. In 1876, M.C. Meeker arrived in Occidental. He became a lumber baron who established several mills in the area. He and Dutch Bill Howard competed for the dominant position in Occidental—each owning much of the town. Meeker also established the community of Camp Meeker, an unincorporated area near Occidental comprised of about 350 homes. (Courtesy Sonoma County Library.)

M.C. MEEKER'S "WHITE HOUSE," 1876. The Victorian home of M.C. Meeker was located off Bittner Road. It used waterpower to generate electricity for lighting and other purposes, like sawing wood. Meeker built a half-mile narrow-gauge railroad to move lumber from the sawmill near his home to the railroad in Occidental. The house was built in 1876 for $10,000 after Meeker's first home was destroyed in a fire in 1872. (Courtesy Harold Lapham.)

TAYLOR FAMILY, C. 1883. Elizabeth McCandless was four years old in 1841 when she left Ireland with her sister for America—she never saw her parents again. Godfrey Taylor, also from Ireland, came to America when he was 14 years old. He married Elizabeth in the 1850s, and they traveled West in oxen-driven wagons. Seen here is the Taylor family, including Martha, Miriam, Thursnelda, Cordelia, Hercules, Godfrey, and Elizabeth. (Courtesy Sonoma County Library.)

BONES FAMILY, C. 1885. William and Salina Bones brought their family from Missouri to Sonoma County in 1862, just after the start of the Civil War. They crossed the plains in a wagon train with their eight children—two others died as infants. Their son William took care of his aging parents until they both died in their early eighties. William, the son, made charcoal and was also successful in the cherry industry. (Courtesy Sonoma County Library.)

LAPHAM FAMILY, 1893. Charles Lapham fought for the Wisconsin infantry during the Civil War and was wounded by a musket ball. He and his younger brother Matthew came to California in 1888. Charles soon moved to Occidental and worked in the sawmills and a variety of other jobs in the area. He and his wife, Delia, had nine children, and seven reached maturity. The photograph shows family members Iva, Ethel, Clyde, Nell, Lynn, Kate, Delia, Coit, and Charles. (Courtesy Sonoma County Library.)

PROCTOR FAMILY, C. 1895. Members of the Proctor family are seen leaving for a camping trip. David and Verlender Proctor established themselves in Occidental in 1883 and raised orchids. Their daughter Effie married W.B. Coy in 1885. Son Walter was an engineer and builder of many homes and bridges in the county. W.B. Coy's store and the Altamont Hotel are visible in the background. (Courtesy Collection of L.W. Proctor.)

GOBETTI FAMILY, C. 1898. The Gobetti family ran the Union Hotel from 1879 to 1887. In 1924, a double funeral was held for Giovanni Gobetti and son-in-law Enrico Brambani, who both fell ill and died within hours of each other. This tragedy resulted in the sale of the Union Hotel to Carlo Panizzera. The photograph shows John Gobetti, Enrico Brambini, Kate (Gobetti Brusa) Cnopius, Joseph Gobetti, Giovanna Gobetti, and Minnie (Gobetti) Brambini. (Courtesy Sonoma County Library.)

GIOVANNI GONNELLA, C. 1900. Giovanni and Teresa (Mucci) Gonnella are common ancestors to all Occidental Gonnellas. Giovanni was born in 1828 in Barga, Italy, and Teresa was born in 1820 in Tiglio, Italy. In 1874, Giovanni started the flow of immigration from that area of Italy to Occidental; his exact reason why is not known. They had five sons and one daughter, and many of the eight generations of their descendants still live in the Occidental area. (Courtesy Frank and Barbara Gonnella family.)

23

DONATI FAMILY. Joe Donati came to Occidental in 1902 from Tuscany, Italy. Brother Dionisio came in 1907 when he was 13 years old, and he peeled tanbark, made charcoal, and became a partner in the Sturgeon Lumber Mill. From left to right are (first row) father Bernardo, adopted girl Nellie ?, and mother Claudina; (second row) John, Dionisio, Carlo, Joe, Giovanni, Theresa, Leontina, Daria, and Dosola. (Courtesy Elizabeth Mazzotti.)

FACENDINI FAMILY. Bartolomeo was the first Facendini to come to Occidental, in 1904. He eventually returned to Italy, but in 1908, his brother Gulliermo moved to Occidental. Gulliermo served in the US Army in World War I. Afterward, he and his wife, Maria, shown here, grew apples and cherries on their ranch on Facendini Lane and sold their produce to local businesses. Their grandchildren Nancy Facendini Burns and Bill Facendini ran the local Occidental Market for 11 years. (Courtesy Facendini family.)

BEEDLE FAMILY, c. 1908. Louis and Charlotte Beedle married in 1852 when she was 14. They had eight children and homesteaded near Occidental in the early 1860s. When Charlotte was 12 years old, she hid away on a ship, where her father was a carpenter, to escape her stepmother. When it arrived in California in 1851, everyone jumped ship looking for gold, but Charlotte was left with friends and never saw her father again. The photograph does not identify these Beedles, but they likely include sons George, Louis, and Louis's wife, Jenny. (Courtesy Sonoma County Library.)

SPECKTER FAMILY, 1910. Richard Speckter was the first of two brothers to come to Occidental. In 1882, he purchased 130 acres in Occidental and grew apples and grapes. In 1885, his brother John followed him. John married Hannah Kling and helped run her family's ranch, and they had a son, Ernest. Richard and John owned the Mound Winery from the 1890s until Prohibition. This photograph at the Speckter ranch shows Harry Grauerholz, Ernest Speckter, Madelaine Meldon, John Speckter, Richard Speckter, Mrs. Meldon, and Henry Grauerholz. (Courtesy Sonoma County Library.)

BRIANS FAMILY, 1912. Benjamin W. and Sarah Brians came to Sonoma County in the 1850s and had eight children, including Benjamin P., pictured here. In 1873, Benjamin W. Brians disappeared, leaving his wife and family. From left to right are dog Trusty, Benjamin P. Brians, Willis Garcia, and Hattie (Bones) Brians. Willis was the son of Alice (Bones) Garcia. Benjamin P. Brians was a lumberman and then opened the first garage in Occidental. (Courtesy Sonoma County Library.)

RUSTY AND RAY GONNELLA, C. 1915. Orestes "Rusty" Gonnella, born in 1897, trapped animals for fur and stripped tanoaks when younger. He was in the Merchant Marines during World War I, but was both homesick and seasick. Dionisio "Ray" Gonnella, born in 1899, was brought up in the Occidental area, moved to the San Francisco Bay Area, and returned in 1938. He was an excellent carpenter. Rusty and Ray were first cousins and friends. They enjoyed joking around, as seen here. (Courtesy Frank and Barbara Gonnella family.)

ILLIA FAMILY, 1915. Innocente Illia came to the United States in 1892 from Italy. His brother Martin continued on to Argentina, where his son Arturo became president of the country. Innocente was a farmhand and met a beautiful Irish woman, Helena Redmond, who was a housekeeper on the ranch next door. Even though they did not speak the same language, they met with lanterns in the backfield and spoke the language of love. They married in 1900 and had five children: Martin, Michael, Stephen, John, and Hilda. They raised cattle on their Coleman Valley School Ranch. (Courtesy Frank and Barbara Gonnella family.)

FRATI FAMILY, 1920. Domenico Frati came to Occidental about 1880 from Tuscany, Italy. His first job was driving teams of oxen for Boss Meeker, and he later acquired land to plant grapes. Domenico and friend Dionisio Gonnella returned to Italy to find wives and returned the next year with them. Domenico and his wife, Zita, had seven children. None of their five sons married, and all worked on ranches throughout their lives. Pictured are five of their children, Peter, Abraham, Helen, Fred, and Angela, along with Domenico Frati and Frank Pieroni. (Courtesy Sonoma County Library.)

BITTNER FAMILY, 1924. Frederick and Helena Bittner came to Occidental in 1881. They had six children: Robert "Bob," Marie Helena, Martha, Nellie, Alma, and Claire. The photograph shows Frederick and Helena with five of the six children at their home, with Bob Bittner holding the white horse. Bob Bittner cut Meeker Road through to Joy Road and renamed it Bittner Road. He also ran a sawmill and became a road commissioner. (Courtesy Harold Lapham.)

EDWARD AND HILDA POZZI, 1925. Luigi Carlos Pozzi immigrated to America in the 1890s. He purchased a 73-acre ranch on Taylor Lane. In 1907, his wife, Carmelina, and young sons Edward and Angelo boarded the *La Lorraine*, crossing the Atlantic to join Luigi in Occidental. In 1917, Luigi died at the age of 51 when a horse, pulling barrels of wine, jumped and crushed him near Joy School. Luigi's son Edward met Hilda Illia (pictured) at a dance in Valley Ford. (Courtesy Teres [Pozzi] Santos.)

MARRA FAMILY, 1928. Battista and Catterina Marra were both born in Switzerland and arrived together in the 1880s. Their family owned and operated a dairy ranch at the end of Marra Road. They had five children, including brothers Charles and John. John's 22-year-old son Loren was a US Marine who drowned in a boating accident at Camp Pendleton in 1955. The photograph shows John Marra in brother Charles's hot rod. (Courtesy Sonoma County Library.)

JOHN AND LEONTINA GONNELLA FAMILY, C. 1949. Giovanni "John" and Leontina Gonnella are seen here with 12 of their 14 children. From left to right are (first row) Louise, John, and Leontina, (second row) Rueben, Dan "McGee," Daria, Eva, Stella, Anna, Claudia, June, Dolores, Ben, and Gildo "Babe." John was an industrious man who worked at various mills in the area. Leontina was an excellent cook, and many of their children returned home every Sunday for a meal. (Courtesy Bob Panizzera.)

RICO CALVI, C. 2003. Rico Calvi was fiercely independent and innovative in mechanical devices. In 1940, he began operating a simple sawmill in Occidental, and he cut and milled walnut and redwood by himself. His father, Jacob, was a bootlegger during Prohibition. Rico and his wife, Emma Rose, had five children. Rico is pictured here when he was 92 years old. A related Calvi family in the area was that of Ceasare and Caterina Calvi. The Calvi families were involved in timber, ranching, and construction. (Courtesy John Calvi family.)

RELIGIOUS CAMP MEETING, 1892. Ministers from various churches would travel between towns on horses or mules and preach to ad hoc congregations. The gatherings could last a week and were both religious and social functions. This gathering was on Occidental Road in Green Valley. (Courtesy Sonoma County Library.)

M. E. Church Occidental, Cal.

METHODIST CHURCH WITH SPIRE, C. 1906. The Methodist church was the first building in town, completed in 1876. The spire and bell tower were added in 1888 but were replaced with a dome after the 1906 earthquake for safety reasons. The church closed its doors in 1972, but it reopened two years later as a nondenominational Protestant community church. (Courtesy Harold Lapham.)

METHODIST EPISCOPAL CHURCH INTERIOR, C. 1891. During the 1888 presidential election between Benjamin Harrison and Grover Cleveland, a $700 bet about the outcome was made between A.P. Meeker and Pat Connolly. Meeker won and told Connolly, "I will buy a bell so you can hear your money ring." The bell still hangs in the church's belfry with the inscription, "Presented by AP Meeker, December 15, 1888." Rev. W.A. Johns is pictured inside the church. (Courtesy Sonoma County Library.)

St. Philip the Apostle Catholic Church, c. 1905. In 1901, Joseph and Julia Asti donated land to build a Catholic church for the token value of one gold coin. The result was a shingle-style building with Victorian Gothic influence. In 1903, the church was dedicated by Archbishop George Montgomery of the Diocese of San Francisco. The house to the left was built by George Proctor and was the residence of Dr. Horace Lamb. (Courtesy Frank and Barbara Gonnella family.)

St. Philip Confirmation, 1917. A group is outside St. Philip Catholic Church after receiving the sacrament of Confirmation. The group includes members of the Marra, Illia, Gonnella, Frati, O'Brian, Panelli, Frugoli, Giovannini, Williams, Drago, Guidici, Belli, Paladini, Pieroni, Mullen, Chiaroni, and Pallette families. (Courtesy Frank and Barbara Gonnella family.)

POST OFFICE, 1910. The Occidental Post Office was dedicated on December 7, 1876, with Andrew Blaney as the first postmaster. The post office was destroyed in the fire of 1924 and rebuilt. Its location, however, moved many times afterward—from inside the W.B. Coy General Merchandise Store, to Togneri's Garage, and several other locations. Blaney was also a coroner and justice of the peace. (Courtesy Sonoma County Library.)

POSTMASTER LOUISE MORELLI, C. 1924. Sisters Louise and Elizabeth Morelli were expelled from Tomales High School when they refused to snitch on their friends who were caught drinking at Dillon's beach. Their father, Joe Morelli, had to pick them up, but he told the principal he was proud of them for not snitching. In 1924, at 19 years old with only a grammar school education, Louise Morelli became one of the youngest postmasters in California. (Courtesy Elizabeth Morelli Perry.)

COLEMAN VALLEY SCHOOLHOUSE, C. 1904. The Coleman Valley Schoolhouse was built in 1864, and represents a typical single-room schoolhouse from this period. In front of the school is Bill Hendren in a buggy with his horse Susie, a former racehorse. (Courtesy Bob Sturgeon family.)

COLEMAN VALLEY SCHOOLHOUSE INTERIOR, C. 1920. Transportation was slow and difficult before the arrival of the automobile, so several small schoolhouses were built around the Occidental area. Light was provided by a bare bulb, and heat was provided from a single wood-burning stove. The school closed in 1941. (Courtesy Sonoma County Library.)

MEEKER SCHOOLHOUSE AND STUDENTS, c. 1918. This schoolhouse on Bittner Road was built in 1879. The school district was initially named the Narrow-Gauge School District, but the name was soon changed to Meeker School District. This was the first school within the town of Occidental. It was abandoned in the early 1920s. (Courtesy Frank and Barbara Gonnella family.)

MEEKER SCHOOL, c. 1918. Teacher Dorothy Percy is shown at far right. Surnames of the students include Thompson, Panelli, Pieroni, Gonnella, Wasson, Guidici, Bones, Lapham, Cox, Franceschi, Giovannini, Lamb, Paladini, Bruce, Chiaroni, and Kingwell. The significance of the students' cat artwork is unknown. (Courtesy Frank and Barbara Gonnella family.)

OCCIDENTAL SCHOOL, 1916. Pictured are students from the Heintz, Garnero, Morelli, Valdez, Chenoweth, Hansen, Bohall, Brush, Pieroni, Bones, Clasley, and Drago families, with teacher Mary Nell Miller. Some of the boys are barefoot, and although it was considered a sign of poverty in the cities, it was more common and acceptable in the country. Mark Twain wrote that boys did it to be tough—"A boy who didn't go barefooted . . . was viewed as a Miss Nelly." (Courtesy Frank and Barbara Gonnella family.)

DRUIDS CEMETERY. Many of the original settlers are buried in Druids Cemetery on Occidental Road. The cemetery was started by Frederick Sieg of the Ancient Order of the Druids, and the first burial was in 1905. Some Catholics in town preferred to be buried elsewhere, such as the Catholic cemetery in Bodega. Norma Piazzo was instrumental in restoring and maintaining Druids Cemetery in 1982. (Courtesy Barbara Gonnella.)

Three

LOGGING AND SAWMILLS

To the early settlers, the number of redwood trees in the Occidental area may have seemed limitless. Hard work was, of course, required to fell, move, and mill the trees, but it seemed that the raw resource would always be there. Before steam and internal combustion engines, the logging and milling process was backbreaking work—typically, two men with a saw would fell the tree and oxen would drag it to a water-powered mill. After a swath of trees was logged, lumber mills sometimes were moved to minimize the distance the logs had to be dragged.

The first lumber mill in the area was constructed in 1859 about a mile south of town. It was run by Mudge, Phelps, and Perkins. M.C. Meeker built a mill in the same area in 1866. By 1877, there were six mills nearby: Meeker's, Glynn's, Tyrone's, Latham and Streeten's, Railroad Land and Lumber Co., and the Madrone Land and Lumber Co. The abundance of large trees produced enough lumber to supply much of the greater San Francisco Bay Area, including rebuilding San Francisco after the devastating 1906 earthquake. By 1890, donkey steam engines replaced draft animals to more easily move the logs. However, all steps of lumbering remained difficult and dangerous. There were continual concerns about falling trees and limbs, controlling logs going down hills, exposed sawblades, and unsafe donkey engines.

Other sawmills soon arose in the area, including Sturgeon's Mill, Fuller's Mill, and Thorpe's Mill. Logging shows were contests held at some sawmills to demonstrate the strength, speed, and agility of the lumberjacks as they performed logging tasks on the enormous trees. The January 3, 1894, *Petaluma Courier* said that M.C. Meeker, chairman of the Sonoma County Midwinter Fair in Occidental, displayed a "redwood 23 feet in diameter, tanbark 8 feet in diameter." People marveled at the enormity of these trees as they began to disappear.

After the devastating fire of 1924, which burned much of the remaining timber near Occidental, and the end of the railroad in 1930, the local commercial lumber industry was almost over. Most of the old-growth trees were either logged or burned, and logging operations were smaller and more selective.

LOGGING BY HAND, 1900. Early logging required that trees be felled by manual sawing. Some of the larger trees, like the one seen here, were sometimes too large to move after being felled. Holes would then be bored into the tree and filled with gunpowder, and the log split before moving. Pictured are Steve Tisconi (left) and Bill Brian. (Courtesy Bob Sturgeon family.)

TURNING OXEN AROUND, C. 1880. It takes considerable skill to maintain control over oxen. Shown are two men in the middle of 12 oxen, turning them around so they could line up and drag a log to the lumber mill. The oxen were sometimes replaced by mules and horses, and eventually, machinery like donkey engines. Oxen were less expensive than mules and horses, and only required a yoke, but they did not have as much judgment or agility. (Courtesy Bob Sturgeon family.)

BULL TEAM, 1893. The man in charge of the oxen, called the "bull-puncher," must control the oxen with a hickory stick and boundless energy. An 1874 book describes the bull-puncher: "He must have a born gift for profanity, or he need never hope to reach high standing in the profession." He was often the highest paid man on a logging crew. Shown is bull-puncher Ira P. Lapham driving Charles E. Fuller's bull team. (Courtesy Sonoma County Library.)

MOVING LOGS DOWNHILL, C. 1900. Moving logs downhill could be dangerous. If control was lost, they could overtake the animals and people. Almost all aspects of logging and milling were dangerous. At Fuller's mill in 1903, according to the *Petaluma Daily Morning Courier*, J. La Franchi's legs were crushed between two logs, and the next year, Edger Joe Palmer lost two fingers when he contacted a saw. These accidents were common, and more newsprint was often devoted to a social visit than to a mill accident. (Courtesy Bob Sturgeon family.)

Meeker Lumber Company, 1885. This lumber company was located on what was then Dixon's Creek, east of Occidental. The mill was bought from Frank M. Gifford in 1876. The man in the doorway is Orrin J. Meeker. The last names of other workers include Motsi, Bones, Stone, Chenoweth, Koffman, Swagard, McCowan, W.S. Procktor, Coy, Brown, and Frati. (Courtesy Sonoma County Library.)

Meeker Brothers Sawmill, 1885. Joe Palmer (third from left) and his wife, Eva Palmer (first woman on the left) are pictured here. Saw blades were exposed, so safety was a constant concern, and accidents were not uncommon. (Courtesy Sonoma County Library.)

GLYNN SAWMILL, 1887. Frank Glynn bought the Jack Smith sawmill in Coleman Valley. He became a Sonoma County supervisor for several terms and was chairman of the board for one term. In 1915, when Glynn was 72 years old, he sat down in the barber's chair for a shave. The barber noticed that he was unusually quiet and discovered that he had died. (Courtesy Sonoma County Library.)

GOING TO DEL MAR MILL, C. 1890. The Glynn and Peterson Mill in Del Mar was north of Occidental. As lumber started to run out in the Occidental area, lumber barons looked farther north, where there were still virgin forests close to the northern terminus of the North Pacific Coast Railroad. These oxen were used for moving the logs. This mill burned down in 1910. (Courtesy Bob Sturgeon family.)

FULLER'S MILL CREW AND CHILDREN, 1890. George Frederick Witham (far left) is pictured with the Fuller's Mill crew and children. Witham was an early pioneer who drove oxen teams at a time when lumber was hand-hewn. In 1898, Charles E. Fuller lost his brother A.A. Fuller when a tree fell on him near Occidental. The *Sonoma West Times and News* reported, "He was hurled into eternity without a moment's warning." (Courtesy Sonoma County Library.)

RAIL SYSTEM AT FULLER'S MILL, 1898. Some of the local mills had a rail system, often made of hardwoods, for transporting logs and lumber near the mills. Shown is Elsie Vanderleith at Fuller's Mill near such a rail system. Her husband, John, was a bookkeeper at Fuller's Mill who lost an arm when his wagon rolled into a ditch in 1901. He was charged with murder in 1910, but he claimed the shooting death was accidental and was acquitted. (Courtesy Sonoma County Library.)

BRIDGE TIMBER FROM FULLER'S MILL, 1896. An 84-foot piece of timber was delivered by Charles E. Fuller to Mark West to build a bridge. Fuller's Mill was south of town. The photograph also shows Stanley Collister, Orion Meeker, Steve Meeker, Dell Pride, Fred Dodge, and Lee Carrels. In the background are the Coy store, Altamont Hotel, and McCandless blacksmith shop. (Courtesy Sonoma County Library.)

WOMEN PULLED BY OXEN, C. 1903. These women are sitting on a log hitched to oxen, making for a dangerous ride. When pulled by oxen, the logs would usually travel along skids of thick branches perpendicular to the direction of travel, called a skid road. The branches were often lubricated with animal fat to reduce friction. (Courtesy Sonoma County Library.)

THE STEAM DONKEY ENGINE, C. 1910. The donkey engine, invented in 1881, is a steam-powered winch that could be used to drag logs toward it. By attaching its cable to a tree or stump, the donkey engine could also move itself. The donkey engine, in conjunction with the railroad, greatly accelerated timber harvesting. Seen here are Ralph Mazzotti and Pete Pretti. (Courtesy Bob Sturgeon family.)

EVOLUTION OF DONKEY ENGINE, C. 1910. The donkey engine replaced animals previously used to move logs. From the 1890s until the 1920s, donkey engines were wood burning. After that, most were oil burning until the late 1930s, when they were replaced by internal combustion engine tractors. A steam donkey engine is pictured with Ralph Mazzotti, Pete Pretti, and other loggers. (Courtesy Bob Sturgeon family.)

FIREWOOD FOR THE RAILROAD, 1911. This tree on the Hendrens' property near Glynn's Camp was felled and split for firewood, possibly for the steam locomotives, although most engines had been converted to oil by this time. A long wooden shoot was built nearby to slide the wood down to railroad cars. Shown are, from left to right, Verner Hendren, "lame" Charlie Rasmussen, Alex Hendren, and Joe McCannon. (Courtesy Bob Sturgeon.)

SUGAR LOAF LOGGING SHOW, 1914. A logging show occurred at Sturgeon's Mill off Coleman Valley Road in July 1914. Logging shows demonstrated strength, speed, and agility as loggers climbed trees, cut logs, and moved them. Logging shows in 1914 would be much different from current logging shows, which may use chainsaws, bulldozers, and logging trucks. (Courtesy Bob Sturgeon family.)

MOVING LOG NEAR THORPE'S SAWMILL, 1924. Jim Thorpe's Atterbury truck is being assisted by four horses to move a log up a grade from Scotty Creek near Thorpe's sawmill, Buckhorn Ranch. As lumbermen transitioned from draft animals to internal combustion engines, this was a way to address the need for additional horsepower. (Courtesy Bob Sturgeon family.)

TRANSPORTING FIR LOG, 1924. Douglas fir is the third tallest tree in the world after redwood and eucalyptus and is found in proximity to coastal redwoods. Fir is quick growing and can live over 500 years. Although redwood can act as a natural insect repellent, fir has a higher strength-to-weight ratio. This fir log is being transported by a truck with solid wheels, which enabled the vehicle to carry more weight at the expense of increased road vibration. (Courtesy Bob Sturgeon family.)

"Sindy" the Steam Donkey, c. 1925. Jim Thorpe and his son are pictured with "Sindy" the steam donkey engine. Thorpe bought the donkey engine from Bob Bittner's mill. When it was moved to Buckhorn Ranch, it was placed in the back of Thorpe's solid-wheel Fageol truck, but because it weighed so much, two men had to sit on the front fenders to keep the truck's front wheels on the ground. (Courtesy Bob Sturgeon family.)

Thorpe Twins Near Lumber Truck, 1928. Identical twins June and Jewell Thorpe lived in an old Coleman Valley ranch home on Fitzpatrick Lane and then at the Buckhorn Lumber Mill on Coleman Valley Road. In this photograph, the lumber from the mill may have been going directly to the San Francisco Bay Area or to the train depot in Occidental where it could then be transferred. (Courtesy Bob Sturgeon family.)

TWO GENERATIONS OF SAWMILL PARTNERS. With a partnership based on a handshake, James Henningsen and Ralph Sturgeon owned and operated the Sturgeon mill from 1943 to 1964. James passed his half of the mill to his son Harvey, and Ralph passed on his interest to his son Bob and daughter Essie Doty. The mill is now a nonprofit working museum that draws thousands of visitors. From left to right are Harvey Henningsen, Jim Henningsen, Ralph Sturgeon, and Bob Sturgeon. (Courtesy James Henningsen.)

PRESERVING THE PAST. In 1993, at a 30-year reunion, seven former Sturgeon mill workers each threw in a $100 bill as a commitment to restore the old steam-powered sawmill. The mill now has demonstrations open to the public. The Sturgeon family and Henningsen family (pictured) were instrumental in this commitment. From left to right are (first row) Jeanie Arneklev and Gail Rhodes; (second row) Jens Henningsen holding Harvey Henningsen, Esther Henningsen, Wilhelmina Henningsen, Jim Henningsen, Sylvia (Henningsen) Fisher (on log), and Ralph Henningsen. (Courtesy James Henningsen.)

Four

RAILROADS AND TRANSPORTATION

Occidental was an isolated community until the railroad came and revolutionized the transportation of people, goods, and mail. The importance of the arrival of the railroad in Occidental in 1876 cannot be overstated because many roads used by horse-drawn wagons were poorly maintained and slow. The original impetus for the railroad was the logging industry, and the railroad allowed a direct and relatively reliable route to San Francisco, which was experiencing a building boom. Before the railroad arrived, products were inefficiently shipped overland via wagons or by water via Tomales Bay.

The narrow-gauge North Pacific Coast Railroad was completed in 1876, connecting the north side of San Francisco Bay to Occidental. Laborers, including many from China, were instrumental in building the railroad, but newspapers of the day reflected a growing racist hostility to the Chinese immigrants. By April 1886, the Chinese in Occidental had moved because of this hostility.

Occidental would temporarily come to a stop each day as travelers were welcomed at the train depot and outside news would arrive. The sound of the train whistle, firebox roaring, and ground rumbling could not be ignored as the train came into town. Lumber, firewood, shingles, tanoak bark, charcoal, dairy, and agricultural products would be loaded onto the train heading back toward San Francisco. The boys in town dreamed of being railroad men, harnessing the power of the hissing and steaming iron horse—but train travel was not always safe, and derailments and other accidents were always a concern.

The Northwestern Pacific Railroad (NWP) "Redwood Empire Route" line was created in 1907 through the consolidation of six separate railroad companies held by the Santa Fe and Southern Pacific Railroads. At one point, the railroad consisted of 60 different companies, which caused difficulties in controlling its finances. Just as the railroad replaced horse-drawn wagons, cars and trucks on better-maintained roads quickly replaced the railroad. The last train left Occidental on March 29, 1930, with a wreath on the front reading, "Gone, but not forgotten." Many were saddened as the sound of the last train whistle leaving Occidental marked the end of an era.

EARLY ROADS, C. 1904. Early roads around the area were rocky and dusty in the summer, and swollen creeks could be dangerous to cross in the winter. But the situation soon changed in Occidental—a letter written by Nancy McCaughey in 1892 reads, "The main street is all graveled, taking all together it looks like an enterprising town, if it were not for the horrible old saloons it would be." This 1904 photograph shows Gene Meeker driving a stagecoach from Occidental to the Petaluma & Santa Rosa Electric Railroad. (Courtesy Sonoma County Library.)

ROAD GRADING, C. 1895. With an increase in the number of people and carriages, more effort was made to improve the roads. A grader uses a long blade to create a flat surface. The earliest graders, like the one shown here, were drawn by horses. By the early 1900s, graders started to be towed by vehicles, and by 1920, a grader could be added as an attachment to a tractor. From left to right are Joah Jonas, Burr Glynn, and George Beedle. (Courtesy Harold Lapham.)

TRANSPORTATION BEFORE THE RAILROAD. Before the North Pacific Coast Railroad operated in Occidental in 1876, the available modes of transportation were walking, horseback riding, or riding in a horse-drawn carriage. The railroad revolutionized the transportation of people, goods, and mail in a short time. In this photograph from 1900 are members of some pioneer Occidental families—the Donatis, Mazzottis, and Gonnellas. (Courtesy Elizabeth Mazzotti.)

CHINESE RAILROAD WORKERS, 1878. About 1,300 Chinese laborers helped build the Pacific Coast Railroad tracks between 1873 and 1876. After the Gold Rush, unemployment rates rose, which contributed to racist hostility toward Chinese immigrants. In 1882, the Chinese Exclusion Act barred further immigration. Many Chinese moved from Occidental in April 1886 after hostile anti-Chinese gatherings there. Shown is an 1878 illustration of Chinese railroad laborers. (Courtesy Sonoma County Library.)

BROWN'S CANYON BRIDGE, C. 1877. Brown's wooden truss bridge, located a half mile south of Occidental, was built in 1876 by the North Pacific Coast Railroad. The tracks were 137 feet above the stream bed and spanned 300 feet. The original bridge had a single post in the middle, called a cluster pier, and was the country's tallest timber bridge. (Courtesy Harold Lapham.)

BROWN'S CANYON TRESTLE, C. 1900. The original truss bridge was later strengthened with trestle work. Shown is a northbound passenger train with engine No. 3 crossing Brown's Canyon trestle. There was an effort in 1976 by railroad enthusiasts to reconstruct the railroad between Freestone and Occidental, but rebuilding the bridge across Brown's Canyon was cost prohibitive. (Courtesy Harold Lapham.)

WAITING FOR PASSING TRAIN, C. 1889. The original Altamont Hotel can be seen on the left and the W.B. Coy General Merchandise Store on the right. This photograph was taken before the devastating fire of 1899. The view is from the end of Coleman Valley Road looking east toward Third Street in Occidental. (Courtesy Harold Lapham.)

TWO ENGINE TRAIN, 1895. A two-engine train is seen in Occidental with a line of passenger cars behind it. A two-engine train, called double heading, was common with steam locomotives to help haul loads up grades and speed the train to maintain schedules. Double heading required careful coordination between engine crews to prevent stalling and derailment. (Courtesy Sonoma County Library.)

Unlucky Locomotive No. 13, 1898. In 1883, a new locomotive was ordered from Baldwin with 10,092 pounds of tractive power—greater than engine No. 8, the previous strongest engine. But No. 13 was soon considered to be an unlucky engine since it was involved in numerous mishaps and fatal accidents. The men shown are Jack Williams, Jack Howard, Ray Roix and Charles Bones. (Courtesy Sonoma County Library.)

First Cab-Forward Locomotive, 1901. NPC No. 21, the first cab-forward engine in the world, was built in Sausalito in 1901. The design allowed the crew to be ahead of the exhaust smoke and steam. However, its weight distribution caused it to be slippery and difficult to operate, and it was nicknamed "the Freak." The man by the crossing sign is Lee Morelli. The boy on the engine step is Bill Roix, who, along with brother Ray, became a locomotive engineer. (Courtesy Harold Lapham.)

HOWARD OR OCCIDENTAL STATION, 1905. In the 1870s, Dutch Bill Howard granted the North Pacific Coast Railroad a right-of-way through his property for a free lifetime train pass and naming the station Howards Station. This could be confusing to train passengers, who expected the name of the station to be the same as the town. The station name was changed to Occidental after Howard's death in 1899. These men are building tracks near the station. (Courtesy Frank and Barbara Gonnella family.)

PREPARATIONS FOR THE TRAIN, 1907. Seen here are the NWP tracks running through town. Note the large stacks of wood adjacent to the tracks. The trains needed to stop frequently to replenish both wood and water. Within a few years, the engines were converted to oil, which could release much more energy than wood. (Courtesy Frank and Barbara Gonnella family.)

N. W. P. Depot at Occidental, Cal.

TRAIN DEPOT, 1908. The Northwestern Pacific Railroad's Redwood Empire Route was instrumental in the growth of Occidental. Shown is engine No. 90 with a southbound passenger train leaving town. This route was created in 1907 through the consolidation of six separate railroad companies held by the Santa Fe and Southern Pacific Railroads. (Courtesy Frank and Barbara Gonnella family.)

WOMEN AT DEPOT, 1909. It is not known whether these women, including Alice Irene Carrillo and Ida K. Johnson, were awaiting train passengers or were passengers themselves, but the train station was the meeting place when the train arrived. Traveling then was considered a luxury, and people often dressed in their best clothes. The depot sign shows Cazadero, the end of the line, at 16.76 miles away, a journey that was about an hour by train. (Courtesy the Sonoma County Library.)

TRAIN WRECK, 1909. On September 24, 1909, a Northwest Pacific train derailed on a cut near Horseshoe Curve between Freestone and Occidental. The photograph shows it was carrying lumber from town. This was not the first accident near Occidental—a May 1889 *Petaluma Courier* article reported, "An engine on the North Pacific railroad exploded near Occidental tearing up track and damaging a water tank." (Courtesy the Sonoma County Library.)

LIFE OF A TRAIN, C. 1910. NWP engine No. 91 operated between 1894 and 1928. In 1918, it jumped the track near Cazadero on the daily passenger route, but fortunately, a huge tree stump prevented the train from turning over. Engine No. 91 was the last narrow-gauge train out of Cazadero in 1928, and it made its final journey in the same year. It was scrapped in 1934. Shown is NWP engine No. 91 at the Occidental depot. (Courtesy Harold Lapham.)

TRACK WALKER, PENSABENE, C. 1920. Ernesto Pensabene was born in Italy in 1880 and came to the United States in 1902. He was a single man employed at a saloon in Occidental. He then became a track walker for the NWP until his death in 1927. This was a lonely job, inspecting railroad tracks usually at night when the trains were not in operation. The track walker would either walk or use a small railway carriage, as shown here, to look for rocks on the tracks and check the integrity of the rails. (Courtesy Frank and Barbara Gonnella family.)

AWAITING THE TRAIN. The woman sitting in front of the train depot among milk cans is Margaret Adams, wife of Giliam Adams Jr. Her mother-in-law was Annie Adams, daughter of William Howard. Milk was commonly transported in 10-gallon galvanized metal cans, and was typically cooled with blocks of ice to prevent spoilage. The Occidental train sign shown here is now displayed in Occidental's Union Hotel. (Courtesy Harold Lapham.)

BOYS ON THE ENGINE, 1929. Boys hung out around the trains with dreams of becoming railroad men. Pasquale Franceschi, Waldo Erickson, and several unidentified boys pose in front of mighty engine No. 145, the largest narrow-gauge locomotive in the world when it was built by Brooks in 1899. A novel smokestack cover could be operated from inside the cab. (Courtesy Sonoma County Library.)

THE LAST TRAIN, 1930. On a sad March 29, 1930, both the last freight train and last passenger train left Occidental. They had been replaced by gasoline-powered internal combustion engine vehicles. The end of the railroad era, which completely transformed the Occidental area in about 50 years, was over. Wreaths were placed on the front of the engine's headlight reading, "Gone, but not forgotten." (Courtesy Sonoma County Library.)

TRANSPORTATION AFTER RAILROAD, 1927. The Atterbury Motor Company manufactured vehicles from 1913 to 1935, offering rugged trucks rated up to seven tons, which could withstand the roads and terrain around the area. This 1927 photograph shows William Thorpe's vehicle hauling a log. Note that the steering wheel was on the right side, as this truck was built before steering wheel locations were standardized in the United States. (Courtesy Sonoma County Library.)

OCCIDENTAL GARAGE, C. 1937. This service station was built on the site of the first service station in town, owned and operated by Ben Brians and destroyed in the 1924 fire. This later station was owned by Tom Graham (right) and partner Slim Jones. The need for gasoline and vehicle servicing grew quickly when the internal combustion engine gained popularity in the 1920s. (Courtesy Harold Lapham.)

Five

COMMERCE

By 1876, M.C. Meeker built a church, hotel, grocery store, and post office, creating an important basis for a town. As the town grew, so did the number of businesses, including saloons, blacksmith shops, merchandise stores, hotels, and restaurants. As new establishments were constructed and others were destroyed by fires and rebuilt, the face of the town was ever-changing. In 1877, after the naming of Occidental Post Office ensured acceptance of the town's new name, the *Thos. H. Thompson & Co. Sonoma County Atlas* described Occidental: "[It] already boasts of a post, express, and telegraph office, a good hotel, general store, blacksmith shop, church . . . The population is about fifty souls."

Logging and other industries related to trees were important commercial ventures for early Occidental. The sights and sounds of the nonstop logging were unavoidable, but the newly arrived Italians saw much more value in the land than just logging. Charcoal was created from discarded branches, wood was chopped and sold for heating and cooking, rich topsoil was gathered and sold to gardening stores, and bark from tanoak trees was stripped for tanning leather.

Wreaths and garlands are still created from redwood shoots during the holiday season. Cars in town are covered with Christmas trees, and families often eat at one of the Italian restaurants as part of an annual family tradition. Perhaps the most famous Christmas trees from Occidental were the massive Douglas firs delivered each year since 1909 to the upscale City of Paris department store in San Francisco, requiring street closures because of their size.

Important agricultural industries near Occidental have included viticulture and wineries, hops, berries, cherries, and apples. Local dairy cows provided milk and cheese. The early settlers, many from Italy, already knew how to farm and ranch in their native countries, and they successfully applied this knowledge and experience in Occidental. Of course, the town was, and still is, best known for its authentic Italian restaurants, which remain an important business.

HANSEN'S BUTCHER SHOP, C. 1890. William Hansen operated a slaughterhouse for his meat market about two miles from town. This photograph was taken prior to the fire of December 31, 1899, when the shop burned with much of the town. From left to right are Walter Proctor, Al Chenoweth, and manager Stephen Meeker. Walter Proctor was an Occidental architect; some of his local houses are still standing. (Courtesy Harold Lapham.)

Montreal, a pioneer house of Occidental, L. Pare, Proprietor.

MONTREAL SALOON, C. 1890. French Canadian Lazare Pare is seen to the right of the doorway wearing a vest. Inside the saloon was a barbershop operated by Leo Carrillo, shown in a white jacket. The bench in front advertises Pastime Plug Tobacco, a sweetened chewing tobacco pressed into blocks. Also pictured are Nelson Drago and C.S. Chenoweth. This building was destroyed by the 1899 fire. (Courtesy Harold Lapham.)

W.B. Coy General Merchandise Store, c. 1890. This was the first store in Occidental, opened in 1877. It was leased to McCaughey and Co. and then bought by William Bela Coy in 1892. The store was destroyed in the fire of December 1899. W.B. Coy was also the postmaster in the 1890s. The *Petaluma Daily Morning Courier* reported that "Postmaster W.B. Coy was charged with tampering with mail"; he was later acquitted. (Courtesy Harold Lapham.)

Taylor Store, 1896. This building was used as a general merchandise store in 1886 by William Freeman Taylor from Nova Scotia. It was destroyed by the 1906 fire, rebuilt, and survived the 1924 fire. It was then used as a grocery store by Oreste Gonnella, as a general store by H.U. Gonnella in 1928, and more recently, as a café and bakery called Howard's Station Café by the Negri family. Shown in the wagon are W.B. Coy and his wife, Effie. The man on the left with the top hat is Freeman Taylor. (Courtesy Bob Sturgeon family.)

Altamont Hotel at Occidental, first class with 29 rooms, rates reasonable, the travelers home. Kept by W. P. Stone.

FIRST ALTAMONT HOTEL, 1877. The first hotel in Occidental was the Altamont, which was opened in December 1876. Altamont, loosely meaning "highest point," was originally called the Summit House and had 29 guest rooms. It was built by Boss Meeker for visitors and men looking for work in the lumber industry and was run by the J.W. Noble family and then A.J. Blaney. The Altamont burned down in the 1899 fire. (Courtesy Sonoma County Library.)

SECOND ALTAMONT HOTEL, 1922. The second Altamont Hotel was built in 1900. It was run for many years by Andrew Blaney's daughter and her husband, John Connolly. The original hotel was two stories, but the photograph shows that another story was added. The Coy store was just to the left, and Gene Cnopius's general merchandise store was to the right. All these buildings were destroyed in the fire of 1924. (Courtesy Harold Lapham.)

THIRD ALTAMONT HOTEL, C. 1938. The third Altamont Hotel was constructed in the early 1930s. It has been owned by several families, including the DeGailles, who offered both French and Italian dinners. The town's telephone switchboard was in its lobby. In 1943, the Fioris bought the Altamont, serving Italian meals, and in the 1980s, Joe Negri Jr. bought the building and opened a Mexican restaurant there. (Courtesy Sonoma County Library.)

MAKING CHARCOAL, C. 1900. The traditional process of making charcoal was brought over by the Italians. What would have been wasted wood was turned into a valuable commodity, and much of it was sold in San Francisco. Great piles of wood are arranged so that a fire bakes the moisture and volatile compounds from the wood in a low-oxygen environment, which creates the charcoal. Charcoal burns hotter, cleaner, and more evenly than wood, and was an important industry until the 1920s. (Courtesy Bob Sturgeon family.)

OCCIDENTAL HALL AND BLACKSMITHING, 1902. This building was constructed to replace the Odd Fellow's Hall after the fire of 1899. Brothers Bob and John McCandless are in front of their blacksmithing shop. A blacksmith had to have the knowledge to forge and repair many metal objects, including horseshoes. The Occidental Hall upstairs was owned by the Native Sons of the Golden West and used for meetings and events. (Courtesy Frank and Barbara Gonnella family.)

BLACKBERRY PICKERS ON TAYLOR RANCH, 1902. Blackberries were a popular export in the early 20th century, and the pickers were paid 3¢ a box in 1902. This same year, a 19-year-old Occidental man, Louis Brush, living at the Taylor Ranch was convicted of burglary. According to the *Press Democrat*, Brush stole dresses and underclothes of Mrs. Crispi and her daughter: "He is a member of a prominent family and his relatives and friends are at a loss to understand why he has placed himself in the unenviable predicament." (Courtesy Sonoma County Library.)

WATERWHEEL GRISTMILL, 1903. Bert Titus is barely visible sitting on top of a waterwheel at a gristmill near Coleman Valley. A gristmill was used for grinding grain into flour and middling. Water-powered grain mills have existed for over 2,000 years, although most modern mills use electricity or fossil fuels for energy. (Courtesy Sonoma County Library.)

TRANSPORTING GRAPES, C. 1904. A wagon of grapes is pictured between a North Pacific Coast Railroad car and a horse-drawn road grader at the Occidental depot. The people include George Beedle, Burr Glynn, Nelson Drago, Noah Jones, and Frank Drago. (Courtesy Sonoma County Library.)

GARIBALDI HOTEL AND SALOON, 1904. In 1886, Alfonso Franceschi bought two houses that had been a small Chinatown. The Chinese, unwanted in the community, had since left. Franceschi moved the houses, joined them together, and made improvements to create the Garibaldi Hotel and Saloon. He named it after Giuseppe Garibaldi, a nationalist Italian general who helped liberate and unite Italy. (Courtesy Harold Lapham.)

ROCHDALE STORE, 1907. This structure was built after the Hansen Building collapsed in the 1906 earthquake. The Rochdale General Merchandise Company was a group of merchants who consolidated for bargaining power in purchasing goods. The window advertises furnishings, boots, shoes, and farm produce. (Courtesy Frank and Barbara Gonnella family.)

DAIRY COW AND CHILDREN, 1907. This photograph, taken on the Speckter Ranch, illustrates the importance of dairy in the area. Milk and cheese were produced locally and exported via the railroad. The children are Mildred Meldon, Ruth Meldon, and Dorothy Sophie Speckter. Dorothy married Jesse Laurence Lapham. (Courtesy Sonoma County Library.)

FEHR'S STORE, 1914. Swiss Jacques "Jakie" Fehr and his Swedish wife, Mathilde "Tillie" Fehr, operated the town jewelery store in 1897. The building was heavily damaged in the 1899 fire and was destroyed in the 1906 fire, weeks before the earthquake. After it was rebuilt, they expanded their business to include watches, clocks, jewelry, cigars, toilet articles, candy, newspapers, ice cream, and sheet music. The store was damaged again in the 1924 fire, but Fehr again rebuilt it and ran the store until 1933. (Courtesy Sonoma County Library.)

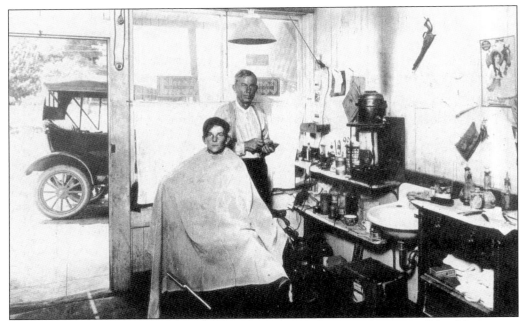

BEN BRIANS'S BARBERSHOP, 1915. Barber Ben Brians is shown with a young John Hausmann. Brians was the uncle of Occidental historian Harold Lapham. This establishment, which included a barbershop, saloon, and a single gas pump, was built at the former site of Lazare Pare's Montreal saloon, destroyed in the 1899 fire. (Courtesy Sonoma County Library.)

MORELLI APPLES, 1916. Apples were once a primary crop of Sonoma County, but many apple orchards have since been replaced by vineyards. In 1910, the Sebastopol Apple Growers Union began what is now called the annual Gravenstein Apple Fair. Some of the oldest apple trees in Sonoma County, planted in 1858, are still located on what used to be the Bittner ranch. Pictured are, from left to right, "Bap," Stella, "Babe," Louise, and Teresa Morelli. (Courtesy Elizabeth Morelli Perry.)

TANBARK TRUCK, C. 1920. Tanbark was cut into four-foot lengths in the spring, left to dry out, and then picked up in the fall. The bark went to tanneries, mainly in Santa Rosa and Vallejo. The photograph shows Ernest Speckter and Irene Gonnella. They married and had no children. (Courtesy Harold Lapham.)

PANIZZERA MEAT COMPANY, C. 1920. The Panizzera Meat Co. was started by Italian immigrants Constante (pictured) and Margaret Panizzera in 1914. Later, their son Joe worked the butcher shop while his wife, Anna (Gonnella) Panizzera, ran the market. In 1971, Joe sold the business to his son Bob who expanded his grandfather's famous sausage production throughout Sonoma County. In 2014, Bob celebrated his family's 100 years in business. (Courtesy Bob Panizzera.)

Employees of Cnopius Merc Co. Occidental Cal [handwritten caption on photograph]

CNOPIUS MERCANTILE COMPANY EMPLOYEES, C. 1920. Owner Eugene Cnopius sold the store to Dionisio Gonnella in 1923, but it burned down in 1924. A temporary airplane lookout structure was built here during World War II. After the war, the Occidental Mercantile Meat Market was built here by Constante Panizzera. It was sold in 1997 to Pat Camilleri and Bill Facendini. Pictured are Sperandio Guidici (on running board), Dionisio Donati (standing in the truck bed), and Dan Chiaroni (sitting in the front seat). (Courtesy Harold Lapham.)

ANSEL BANKS'S CHERRY ORCHARD, 1921. Ansel W. Banks created the El Central Orchard Company and planted 70 acres of cherries and 40 acres of apples. The Sebastopol Apple Growers Union honored Ansel for his methods in pruning, fertilization, and cultivation of orchards. The *Press Democrat* reported in 1942 that girls from Tamalpais High School helped there with the harvest during the war, "combining vacations and victory work." The photograph shows Banks working in his orchard. (Courtesy Thompson family.)

INTERIOR OF GONNELLA STORE, C. 1925. John A. Gonnella and his wife, Theresa, were both born in Italy—John in 1877 and Theresa in 1874. They operated a general store selling groceries, candy, and tobacco. They later added hardware, yardage, notions, a barber shop, and a bake shop. John A. Gonnella is pictured with two of his children, Rose (left) and Daria. The stock includes cooking pots, plates, fabric, and canned goods. (Courtesy Sonoma County Library.)

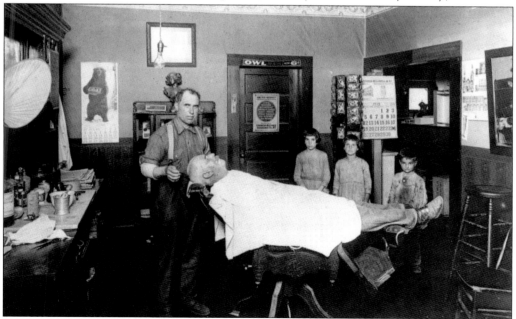

JOHN GONNELLA BARBERSHOP, 1925. John and Theresa Gonnella had a barbershop inside their general store. The cost of a shave in 1925 was about 25¢, and a haircut was about 50¢. Pictured are barber John Gonnella, Carlo Coli in the chair, and Gonnella children (from left to right) Daria, Rose, and Louie. (Courtesy Harold Lapham.)

VERA'S SWEET SHOP, 1933. Elvira "Vera" and Leo Sartor are shown behind the counter at this ice cream parlor and newsstand. Ice cream parlors and soda fountains had been popular in the area since the late 1800s. In 1935, Elvira Sartor was named the arch druidess for the Occidental Circle of Druids. The Druids were not based on a pagan religion; rather, its members were expected to practice the Druid attributes of justice, benevolence, and friendship. (Courtesy Sonoma County Library.)

JOHN GONNELLA GENERAL STORE, 1933. Within this building were a shaving parlor, Italian grocery, and shoe repair. In addition, H.U. Gonnella and Sons Plumbing and Electrical originally operated here. After the railroad stopped, the old depot was used for some years as a warehouse for the store and electrical business. Pictured outside the store are Leo Sartor, Louie Gonnella, John Gonnella, Joe Donati, and Virgil Taddeucci. (Courtesy Sonoma County Library.)

H.U. Gonnella and Sons Store, 1934. Humbert Ulysses Gonnella was born in Italy in 1878 and came to the United States when he was 13 as an indentured servant. He came to Occidental in 1894, and eventually became the owner of a grocery store that also sold electrical and plumbing supplies. In 1901, he married Theresa Franceschi, and they had six children. A group of unidentified men and boys is seen here outside the store. (Courtesy Sonoma County Library.)

Pete Buonaccorsi's Garage, 1938. With the proliferation of internal combustion vehicles, more service stations were needed to provide fuel and keep the often temperamental vehicles running. This service station, shown with a 1930 Buick in front, was Pete Buonaccorsi's Garage. Flying A gasoline was sold along with Cycol oil and local honey. Buonaccorsi was also known for being able to locate hard-to-find underground water. (Courtesy Sonoma County Library.)

JOHN GONNELLA BAKERY TRUCK, C. 1945. John A. and Theresa Gonnella operated a general store, and from 1923 to 1942, owned a bakery where the Occidental Hardware store is now. During the Depression, no funds were available for a new school, so John Gonnella had one built and rented it to the county for a few years before selling it to them in 1935. (Courtesy Harold Lapham.)

MORELLI WINERY, 1948. This successful winery was started in 1913, but Prohibition was a difficult time for all wineries. Dennis Morelli said, "According to family lore, my grandfather cried when the Feds used axes to break open the tanks and let the wine run down the hill by the winery. He vowed that he would never make wine again." Shown here is Dennis Morelli's great-uncle Lee Morelli. The Morelli Winery was sold in 1969. (Courtesy Dennis Morelli.)

WREATHS AND GARLANDS. Two Gonnella brothers, Ermenegildo and Dionisio, started the Occidental redwood wreath and garland business in the late 1800s. For two months before Christmas, many Italians in town worked making these holiday decorations. In 1977, mainly through the efforts of Ben Gonnella, more than 100,000 wreaths were purchased by Boys Republic, a Southern California boys' home, which decorated and sold them as a fundraiser. The men in the photograph are unidentified. (Courtesy Harold Lapham.)

ALFONSO VACCAREZZA WITH WREATHS. Wreaths and garlands were made from second-growth suckers cut from around the redwood stumps. Shown is Alfonso Vaccarezza (near cab), as well as two unidentified boys, ready to deliver a truckload of wreaths. Alfonso Vaccarezza was born in Italy in 1889. He was involved in the nursery and Occidental wreath and garland industry until his death in 1954. (Courtesy Frank and Barbara Gonnella family.)

"MAHONEY" GONNELLA WITH WREATH. Dan Gonnella (pictured) had a cousin and close friend with the same name. To avoid confusion, he assumed the nickname "Mahoney" after Boston Red Sox player Dan O'Mahoney. The other Dan Gonnella was then given the nickname "McGee," perhaps after Boston Braves player Dan McGee. The names stuck. Mahoney's barn was used by cousin Ben Gonnella to make wreaths. (Courtesy Frank and Barbara Gonnella family.)

CITY OF PARIS CHRISTMAS TREE, 1970. From 1850 to 1972, the City of Paris Dry Goods Company was a San Francisco institution. Since 1909, a Christmas tree, up to 60 feet tall, was placed in its rotunda during the holiday season. In 1953, the *San Francisco Chronicle* reported, "For the past 48 years A. Vaccarezza, a woodsman from Occidental, has selected the Douglas Fir for the City Of Paris. The police stopped traffic on Geary St while the tree, sheathed in burlap, made its grand entrance into the City of Paris." (Courtesy Library of Congress.)

Six

CAMPING AND RECREATION

In the early 20th century, the beauty, seclusion, and temperate climate of the area made Occidental a summer destination for many families from the urban congestion of San Francisco. Creeks would be dammed and turned into swimming holes, and picnic areas would be developed nearby. Early campers would hunt, fish, and set up tents or other rustic accommodations under the redwoods.

Several more formal camps were created nearby, often on a religious basis. St. Dorothy's Rest is a summer home for chronically ill children founded in 1901 by Nellie Lincoln and her husband, Rev. James Lincoln, after their eight-year-old daughter Dorothy died of meningitis. Alliance Redwoods was started in 1946 by the Christian & Missionary Alliance, and its rustic camping has evolved into a youth outdoor program and retreat center. Westminster Woods started as land deeded to the Presbyterian Church in 1949 and has evolved from a children's summer camp into a facility camp and conference center. Our Lady of the Redwoods Catholic Camp was dedicated in 1952, and gave children from different socioeconomic backgrounds a camping experience in a natural environment. All these camps have since grown and evolved into year-round retreat centers.

A different kind of camp is the Bohemian Grove, purchased in 1899 by the San Francisco Bohemian Club from lumber baron M.C. Meeker. The property is a restricted 2,700-acre campground, including 160 acres of old-growth redwoods. The Bohemian Club is a private gentlemen's club that still hosts some of the most influential men in the world, including business leaders, US presidents, and prominent artists and musicians.

Because the area has preserved its natural beauty and charm, camping and outdoor recreation experiences are still popular in the Occidental area, a welcome change for many from a hectic urban environment.

San Francisco Cal. march 11, 1906
Dear Marion: I enjoyed your visit very much
When are you coming over? O never say it when
I don't mean it) Lovingly Lois Lyon.

CAMP TYRONE, 1906. The success of Camp Meeker and Monte Rio at the turn of the 20th century encouraged other developers in the Russian River area. Camp Tyrone was a development owned by the Moore Land Company between Camp Meeker and Monte Rio on Austin Creek. In 1904, lots there were selling for $10. This photograph shows a group of girls in the creek at Camp Tyrone. (Courtesy Sonoma County Library.)

Scene in Altamont Park, Occidental, Cal.

ALTAMONT PARK, 1906. This camping and picnic spot was on Salmon Creek just south of town near Scouts Camp Road. The creek was dammed to create a swimming hole. This area is now part of the Catholic Youth Organization (CYO) campgrounds. (Courtesy Sonoma County Library.)

DEER HUNTING. Although there was deer hunting in the Occidental area, many hunting trips were planned farther north where deer were more plentiful. Pictured outside Pete Buonaccorsi's Garage are, from left to right, Amadeo Parnelli, Pete Buonaccorsi, Pasquale Franceschi, and Bob Fiori. (Courtesy Sonoma County Library.)

FISHING AND PICNICKING, 1907. People from Occidental went to the nearby beaches for both fishing and picnicking. These Occidental residents at a local beach are, from left to right, (first row) Stephen Meeker, Stephie Meeker, Kate Meeker, Mrs. Shaw, Sara Meacham, Will Meacham, and Mary Menary; (second row) Harvey Taylor, Tom Menary Jr., John Menary, Bill Harrington, Will Menary, and Charlie Chaplin. (The last name is likely local resident Charles Chapman.) (Courtesy Sonoma County Library.)

BOHEMIAN GROVE, 1929. The Bohemian Grove is a 2,712-acre campground, purchased in 1899 and located between Occidental and Monte Rio. It is owned by a private gentlemen's club known as the Bohemian Club, which hosts some of the most wealthy and prominent men in the world, including top business leaders and US presidents, but also artists and musicians. The names listed on this photograph are Kent, Purington, Mason, Dobie, Finks, Crocker, Harris, and Hook. (Courtesy Sonoma County Library.)

BOHEMIAN GROVE "HIGH JINKS," 1929. Elaborate productions, such as this presentation of *Robin Hood*, are performed as part of the annual Bohemian Grove's High Jinks ceremony. Old-growth redwoods are still on the property, and even in 1882, the *Petaluma Weekly Argus* expressed concerns about the uncontrolled logging: "Bohemian club . . . are about the last big trees near railroads and something ought to be done to preserve them." (Courtesy Sonoma County Library.)

ST. DOROTHY'S REST, C. 1905. This is the oldest continuously operated camp in California, founded in 1901 with land donated by Melvin Meeker. The camp, located at Camp Meeker, was originally a summer home for chronically ill children, founded by Nellie Lincoln and her husband, Rev. James Lincoln (pictured), after losing their eight-year-old daughter Dorothy to meningitis. (Courtesy St. Dorothy's Rest.)

ST. DOROTHY'S REST CHAPEL, C. 1905. In 2012, the 16-acre camp expanded by 550 acres toward the coast through a gift by a camp alumni family. The camp is now a year-round retreat center, hosting groups of teachers and artists. Shown here is Rev. James Lincoln in front of the chapel. (Courtesy St. Dorothy's Rest.)

EARLY CYO CAMP. In the early 1930s, Fr. John V. Silva purchased 12 wooded acres on Salmon Creek and transformed the former Druids Picnic Park into a wilderness camp primarily for teenage boys. Father Silva donated this land to the CYO in 1946. It developed the land into a camp for children, named Our Lady of the Redwoods, in 1952. This photograph shows Salmon Creek dammed to create a swimming hole before two permanent pools were later installed nearby. (Courtesy Catholic Charities CYO Camp.)

CYO CAMP EVOLUTION, C. 1965. Msgr. Peter Armstrong was instrumental in raising funds for expanding acreage and developing the camp to create a year-round facility. In 1969, the new facility was dedicated by and named after Archbishop McGucken. Our Lady of the Redwoods (the older camp) housed the girls, and the new camp housed the boys for a total of about 450 campers each session. Here, Monsignor Armstrong is promoting the new McGucken Center with Archbishop McGucken at center. (Courtesy Catholic Charities CYO Camp.)

ALLIANCE REDWOODS BEGINNINGS, 1963. In 1946, Christian & Missionary Alliance pastors purchased 76 acres. Volunteers, including 80 from the Oakland Neighborhood Church, built the rustic camp. In 1949, $8,000 was borrowed to build Madrone Lodge. Today, Alliance Redwoods includes youth outdoor education programs, a retreat center, and a zip line canopy tour. This 1963 photograph shows people lining up for a meal at the old dining hall. (Courtesy Alliance Redwoods.)

ALLIANCE REDWOODS CRISIS AND RENEWAL, 1965. By 1965, the camp needed substantial work but had only $117 in its treasury, and the county threatened to shut it down. Money from lumber and a loan allowed the camp to continue. The tent frame cabins, which used mattresses donated from a *Queen Mary* ship renovation in the 1960s, were torn down. In 2009, a $7.5 million loan enabled Alliance Redwoods to be revitalized. This photograph shows a 1965 summer camp group with its tent cabins and a water tank in the background. (Courtesy Alliance Redwoods.)

WESTMINSTER WOODS, 1957. In 1940, Rose and Wesley Harrah deeded land, now called Westminster Woods, to the First Presbyterian Church of Pendelton. A gift from E.F. and Martha Terney helped fund improvements to the property in order to provide a home for their disabled daughter in their later years. This photograph shows the newly completed swimming pool, which is still in use today. (Courtesy Westminster Woods.)

WESTMINSTER WOODS CHANGES, C. 1970. In 1993, a recommendation was made to change the facilities from a summer camp to a year-round facility and conference center. Westminster Woods includes hiking trails, a community playground, and a heated swimming pool. This old NWP train tunnel on the property was filled in during the 1990s. (Courtesy Westminster Woods.)

Seven

FAMOUS ITALIAN RESTAURANTS

The earliest settlers were a mix of immigrants from many countries, including Ireland, England, Denmark, Canada, and China. From the 1880s to the 1920s, an increasing number of immigrants came from a few areas in Italy. These Italians were self-sufficient—the women raised farm animals and farmed, while the men sometimes worked freelance, often in the lumber industry. Members of Italian families acted as a team, understanding the need for hard work as a buffer to the possibility of an uncertain economic future. By 1880, Italian immigration was encouraged because of the anti-Chinese sentiment and the need for laborers, and more Italians soon arrived. By 1907, there were 300 Italians in the area, but anti-Chinese sentiment was sometimes replaced with a growing anti-Italian sentiment.

Early Occidental was isolated enough and Italian enough that it could seem much like a misplaced Italian village. The Italians brought with them the skills needed not only to farm but to turn fresh produce and meat into Italian cuisine. The history of the Italian restaurants in Occidental can be traced back to the first Italian settlers before the turn of the 20th century, and by 1900, Occidental was already becoming known for these restaurants. After railroad service stopped in 1930, there was an economic decline in Occidental associated with the Great Depression affecting the entire United States. The primary attraction in Occidental during and after this time remains its Italian restaurants. Generations of visitors identified Occidental as the town with the three famous family-style Italian restaurants—Negri's, Fiori's, and the Union Hotel. Each one had its specialties and faithful patrons, and all had authentic Italian food.

The Union Hotel is the oldest of the three, constructed in 1879 and previously named the Gobetti Union Saloon, likely in honor of the final unification of Italy in 1871. Fiori's Restaurant, previously named the Altamont, was bought by Tony and "Mama Clara" Fiori in 1942. Negri's Restaurant was originally named the Garibaldi Saloon, then Village Café, and finally, Occidental Restaurant; it was bought by Joe Negri Sr. in 1948. The two remaining restaurants, the Union Hotel and Negri's, still serve Italian cuisine, but they now also serve as hubs for the community.

Golden Gate Hotel. This hotel was in the same building as the Good Friend's Saloon. John Gobetti served the first Italian-style meal here for 35¢ on Saturday nights. The hotel was taken over by Narciso "Cheeso" Coli in 1935. In 1959, the building was sold to Carlo and Mary Panizzera, who demolished it to build the Union Motel, which closed in 2003. (Courtesy Frank and Barbara Gonnella family.)

Gobetti Union Saloon, c. 1900. This building was constructed in 1879 by Amelia Jones, who bought the lot from William Howard for $150 and sold it back to him with an empty building for $1,000 one year later. The first floor of this building was a general merchandise store run by Aaron Greenbaum, and the upper level was a public hall. Howard sold the building to the Gobetti family in 1891 for $2,000 in gold. They ran it as the Union Saloon in 1887 and renamed it the Union Hotel in 1891. They operated it until 1925, when they sold it to Carlo Panizzera. (Courtesy Frank and Barbara Gonnella family.)

UNION HOTEL, C. 1940. The Union Hotel ran a boardinghouse for railroad crews; their wives and families would stay there for the day to be picked up on the return run. One morning, waitress Mary Alberigi was carrying a load of linens down the steep stairs at the Union Hotel and tripped. Carlo Panizzera found her and brought her to the doctor, and they were inseparable thereafter. They married in 1929 and had one child, Lucille, in 1930. (Courtesy Frank and Barbara Gonnella family.)

THE HEART OF THE UNION, 1942. Shown are some of the dedicated women who have served generations of families, especially old-time San Franciscans. The recipes of the hand-crafted ravioli and tortas are over 100 years old. From left to right are unidentified, Clorinda Franceschi, Marjorie Gonnella, Lucille Gonnella, Mary Panizzera, and Elizabeth Mazzotti. (Courtesy Frank and Barbara Gonnella family.)

MARY PANIZZERA, 1955. Mary Panizzera is responsible for much of the Italian cuisine still served at the Union Hotel. She was one of the most loved and respected people in town, and *Press Democrat* columnist Gaye LeBaron described her control over the kitchen and loss to the community, saying she had "a silk glove over an iron fist . . . all of Occidental, young and old, hippie and Italian, rancher and counterculture, cried when Mary died." Mary Panizzera is shown here with grandchildren Michael and Mary Theresa Gonnella. (Courtesy Frank and Barbara Gonnella family.)

CHANGES AT THE UNION HOTEL, C. 1955. The hotel portion ended with the end of the railroad about 1929, but it continued as a restaurant and saloon. Mary and Carlo Panizzera cooked on a wood-burning stove; Carlo was against changing to an oil-burning stove because he was worried that it would affect the taste. Their daughter Lucille married Mahoney Gonnella in 1949. They had five children— Michael, Mary Theresa, Mark, Daniel, and Frank. Mahoney died in 1992, and Mark died in 2007. (Courtesy Larry and Linda Priest.)

ALTAMONT "REAL FRENCH & ITALIAN DINNERS," C. 1940. The Altamont at the time of this photograph was owned by George LaCoste, and the town switchboard was located in its lobby. The restaurant was sold in 1942 to Tony and "Mama Clara" Fiori after they sold the Golden Gate Hotel. From left to right are Eleanor Travaglini, Lillie (Baldrini Otte) Provost, Audrey Briggs, Shirley ?, Betty ?, and Thelma (Pelletti) Fernandez. (Courtesy Eleanor Travaglini.)

ALTAMONT COOKS AND WAITRESSES, C. 1945. After Tony and Mama Clara Fiori bought the Altamont, they renamed it Fiori's Restaurant. After 1945, the restaurant was sold to George and Edna Fiori and Raymond and Virginia Fiori. These cooks and waitresses are, from left to right, Mary Fiori, Agnes Clark, Edna Fiori, and Nancy Franceschi. (Courtesy Tami Fiori Mesenbrink.)

FIORI'S RESTAURANT, 1957. George Fiori ran the bar, and Ray Fiori ran the kitchen. After Tony Fiori's death in 1969, the restaurant was sold to Anthony and Irene Buonaccorsi and Bob and Marilou Ranch. They continued to operate it as Fiori's until the 1980s, when the restaurant went out of business. After a few years of closure, the Negri family bought it and reopened it as the Altamont Bar and Grill. (Courtesy Frank and Barbara Gonnella family.)

GEORGE FIORI AT THE BAR. George Fiori was a US Marine veteran who ran for Sonoma County supervisor in 1964. He was sometimes called the unofficial "mayor of Occidental" and was nicknamed the "Black Stallion." Over his bar were several birds used by Alfred Hitchcock when he made his movie masterpiece *The Birds*. Once, four-star general "Howlin' Mad" Holland, Fiori's commander, came into the bar and jokingly gave him a hard time. Fiori did not recognize him, but he was floored when he finally learned his identity. (Courtesy Tami Fiori Mesenbrink.)

FIORI KITCHEN, C. 1950. Ray Fiori ran the restaurant kitchen, but the whole family was involved in ensuring a smooth operation. *Press Democrat* columnist Gaye LeBaron wrote, "There was a continuous fritter debate in the early days. Mary's zucchini fritters were hands-down in the vegetable department. But Raymond Fiori's apple fritters may have edged the Union's banana variety." From left to right are Agnes Clark, Clara Fiori, George Fiori, Raymond Fiori, George Fiori Jr., Virginia Fiori, Edna Fiori, Moby Gonnella, Corinda Fiori, and Harriett Clark. (Courtesy Tami Fiori Mesenbrink.)

GARIBALDI SALOON, 1932. The diary of Wade Sturgeon recalled how John Gonnella and Robert Bittner were backers of the first telephone line into town, which came into the Garibaldi Hotel. Many people gathered around for the first call, and Alfonso Franceschi answered it. The caller spoke in Italian, and Alfonso's mouth fell open as he dropped the receiver, exclaiming, "Dio Mio, it speaks Italian!" This photograph was taken on a rare day with snow. (Courtesy Harold Lapham.)

VILLAGE CAFÉ, 1938. Dionisio "Raymond" and Eleanor (Dinucci) Gonnella bought the Garibaldi Hotel in 1938, remodeled it, and renamed it Village Café. It had one of the first jukeboxes in town. In 1942, it was sold to Virgil Franceschi. It was destroyed by fire in 1945 but was rebuilt and called the Occidental Restaurant. It was then leased to Pete Fiori and Pat Gisler. The building was sold to Joe Negri Sr. in 1948. (Courtesy Harold Lapham.)

NEGRI'S RESTAURANT BEGINNINGS. Joe Negri Sr. was born in 1897 in Venice, Italy, and immigrated to the United States where he was a chef at the famed Waldorf-Astoria Hotel in New York. He moved west and met his future wife, Theresa Tesconi, and moved to Occidental in 1938. Negri worked as a bartender at the Altamont and leased the Union Hotel for a couple years until they purchased what would become Negri's Restaurant. The photograph is from 1963. (Courtesy Harold Lapham.)

Evelyn and Joe Negri Jr., Christmas 1953. Theresa Negri cooked and Joe ran the bar. They had two sons, Joe and Albert. Joe Sr. always had a joke for the patrons and a quarter for the children as he passed through the dining room. Joe Jr. met his future wife, Evelyn Rossini, while working. According to a *Press Democrat* article, Evelyn said, "I was doing glassware and silverware and he was washing dishes." Joe Jr. and Evelyn are shown celebrating their engagement. (Courtesy Amanda Negri.)

Changes at Negri's. When Joe Negri Sr. died in 1970, Joe Jr. took his father's place at the bar. Albert ran the kitchen with his mother, Theresa, and Joe Jr.'s wife, Evelyn. Joe Jr. was devoted to both the restaurant and his racehorses, and drinks were on the house when his horses won. He was also a star athlete, signed to play football with the San Francisco 49ers, but had to quit when his father was sick and could not run the restaurant. (Courtesy Amanda Negri.)

NEGRI'S KITCHEN, LATE 1990S. Negri's featured rock and blues music in its bar in the 1970s and 1980s, along with its authentic Italian cuisine. Joe Negri Jr. and Evelyn had three children, Terry, Joe III, and Sandy. Joe III died in 2005, and Joe Jr. died in 2011. Evelyn and daughter Sandy now run the restaurant with help from grandchildren and other family. Shown is Evelyn Negri making her traditional Italian minestrone soup. (Courtesy Evelyn Negri.)

MOTHER'S DAY C. 1940. Raymond Fiori recalled when the Russian River crowd descended on the town every three-day weekend. The restaurants could not handle all the people, so they would put their names in at all three Italian restaurants and eat at whichever one called them first. It was not unusual to wait two or three hours for dinner. Fiori added, "Our peak day was in 1961, Mother's Day, we served 2,022 dinners. The next day we served 14." (Courtesy Harold Lapham.)

Eight

PATRIOTISM

Patriotism in Occidental started before the town's beginning in 1876, the centennial year of the United States. This patriotism is evident in many vintage photographs from Occidental's early history, where American flags are proudly and prominently displayed. The early immigrants appreciated the opportunities they had in their new land. The most important event of the year in Occidental was on the Fourth of July, when there was live music and food to celebrate the founding of America. According to the 1898 *Sonoma West Times and News* discussing the upcoming Fourth of July picnic, "Native Sons of Occidental erected an 80-foot flag staff. A barbequed ox and 4 sheep."

Some Italians in Occidental were conflicted when the United States entered World War II. They realized that they could have sons and relatives fighting on the US side against other relatives on the Italian side. But many Occidental Italians fought, and some gave their lives, during the war. Ethnic Italians with American nationality were not sent to internment camps like the Japanese, although there were camps for Italian nationals captured in the United States during the war.

After World War II, annual Veterans Day parades and barbecues in Occidental provided a way to honor those who served the United States during the war. Occidental, along with the rest of the country, was relieved that the horrors of the war were over, and the town was eager to celebrate victory and peace.

The 1960s and 1970s were difficult times for most of the country, including Occidental. For the first time since World War II, the meaning of patriotism became unclear—were patriots the soldiers who bravely fought for the United States or those who protested what they perceived as an unjust war in Vietnam? During this time, a veterans' memorial park was built in Occidental, but it did not display a planned memorial plaque for the World War II veterans, likely because of the turbulent political environment. The memorial plaque created for the park was instead stored for over 20 years until 1995, when it was retrieved and placed in front of the flagpole at the Occidental fire station.

RAILROAD MEN WITH AMERICAN FLAG, 1902. The history of patriotism runs deep in Occidental, and there are many stories and celebrations where this has been evident. The immigrants appreciated the opportunities they had in their new land and were proud to show it. This photograph was

taken on July 4, 1902. Early displays of patriotism like this were common. Behind the train and depot is the Depot Saloon, with Alfonso Franceschi listed as proprietor. (Courtesy Frank and Barbara Gonnella family.)

PATRIOTIC SYMBOLISM, C. 1921. One way that new immigrants showed their patriotism was by displaying the US flag—17 flags are visible here. The flyer on the right advertises the MacDonough Show, a local acting troupe that performed in the early 1920s. The people in the bar are, from left to right, Mr. and Mrs. George Lacoste, Alfonso Franceschi, Frank Ward, and Bob Bittner. This photograph was likely taken at the second Altamont Hotel. (Courtesy Frank and Barbara Gonnella family.)

EUGENE VACCAREZZA, C. 1943. Out of the 62 Occidental veterans who served in World War II, two never returned. Eugene Vaccarezza served in the US Marine Corps, and he remains one of 514 soldiers missing in action from the 1943 Battle of Tarawa in the Pacific theater, considered the toughest battle in Marine Corps history. More than 1,000 troops were killed and 2,000 wounded in only three days of fighting. Army private Eugene Rossi was the other World War II soldier who died in the war, of battle wounds at Okinawa. (Courtesy Marjorie Vaccarezza Gonnella.)

"TAYLOR" AND "MAHONEY," C. 1943.
Louis Gonnella was known as "Taylor," and
Dan Gonnella was "Mahoney." The origin
of the nickname Taylor was that another
child said to Louis Gonnella, "You are one
of the Taylor kids, aren't you?" He denied
it, but somehow the name stuck. Shown is
Taylor Gonnella (left) shaking hands with
soldier Mahoney Gonnella. Mahoney was
the first soldier from Occidental to go to
war and the last to come home. (Courtesy
Frank and Barbara Gonnella family.)

VICTOR AND FRANK MORELLI, C. 1943.
During World War II, Victor Morelli (right)
was aboard a ship when it was sunk by a
German bomb, causing the largest loss of
men at sea during the war. About 1,200
died, and only 700 survived the attack.
Although he could not swim, he had on a
life jacket and was knocked unconscious by
flying debris. Frank Morelli (left) was in the
Army infantry and participated in several
landings, including Okinawa. He was also
wounded and received a purple heart. After
the war, the brothers worked the next 20
years in logging. (Courtesy Dennis Morelli.)

HOWARD RESPINI, 1945. Howard Respini was a Navy mechanic responsible for dropping off soldiers and supplies from a landing ship. During one drop-off, they could not unload due to enemy gunfire. There was a US tank on the beach, which soon raised its barrel up toward the trees and killed the sniper. The tank then turned toward Respini's boat and moved its barrel up and down to signal that they could now unload. Howard Respini returned to Sonoma County and reunited with his brothers Jim and Paul, who also served in the war. Howard (seated) is shown with three unidentified sailors. (Courtesy Brad Respini.)

PATRIOTIC POST OFFICE, C. 1945. The Occidental Post Office was a small building sandwiched between the Altamont Restaurant and Gonnella's market during World War II. The windows of the post office during the war were covered with notices to "Cooperate with your Local Defense Council" and to buy war bonds to help finance the war. (Courtesy Sonoma County Library.)

Joe Lunardi, 1945. Joe Lunardi enlisted in the Navy after graduating midterm from Tomales High School, where he was captain of the football team and a baseball star. Lunardi married Doris Gonnella, president of the American Legion Auxiliary and president of the fire department auxiliary. After the war, he was the commander of the local American Legion, chaired the Occidental veterans' picnic, and was Occidental fire chief for 18 years. Lunardi (right) is shown with Art Vincent celebrating the end of the war in Times Square. (Courtesy Harold Lapham.)

The Boys from Occidental, c. 1946. Eleanor Travaglini said she took this photograph of local soldiers on a day that had a parade and barbecue. From left to right are Leigh Thompson, Earl Beedle, Domonic Travaglini, Ned Fiori, and Joe Lunardi. Leigh Thompson was a heavy equipment operator for Sonoma County. (Courtesy Eleanor Travaglini.)

DOMONIC TRAVAGLINI, 1949. Domonic Travaglini served with the US Navy in World War II. When he returned, he worked for Pacific Gas & Electric for 30 years. His wife, Eleanor, was an aircraft spotter during the war and was a longtime correspondent for the *Sebastopol Times*, writing the Occidental column. Shown is Domonic holding a flag at a parade in Occidental. (Courtesy Eleanor Travaglini.)

PLANE SPOTTER ELEANOR TRAVAGLINI. After the Pearl Harbor bombing in 1941, the Army Air Forces Ground Observer Corps was established to perform air raid drills and manage plane spotter towers. The plane spotter towers were furnished with a telephone, binoculars, and information to help identify the direction and types of planes. These posts were staffed by volunteers 24 hours a day, 7 days a week. In this recent photograph, Eleanor Travaglini displays her plane spotter armband identification used during the war. (Courtesy Eleanor Travaglini.)

OCCIDENTAL SAILORS—VICTORY AND RELIEF, C. 1946. This photograph of local sailors was taken by Eleanor Travaglini at an Occidental parade after World War II had ended. From left to right are (first row) Alvin Panelli and Harold Lapham; (second row) Domonic Travaglini, Dario Montafi, and Louis Pelletti. (Courtesy Eleanor Travaglini.)

GRISWALD GIRLS IN VETERANS DAY PARADE, 1954. These girls, believed to be sisters Susan and Judy Griswald, are riding cows in the annual Veterans Day parade. Parades were an important way to honor veterans. This day, originally called Armistice Day, was created after World War I to celebrate the bravery and sacrifice of all US veterans. (Courtesy Harold Lapham.)

OCCIDENTAL AMERICAN LEGION FLOATS. The American Legion is a patriotic veterans' organization devoted to mutual helpfulness. It mentors youth, advocates patriotism and honor, and promotes strong national security. Occidental Post No. 651 of the American Legion entered a float in a parade in Santa Rosa, complete with a soldier and Lady Liberty. (Courtesy Harold Lapham.)

WORLD WAR II VETERANS' PLAQUE. A plaque dedicated to World War II veterans from Occidental was created for a veterans' memorial park in the early 1970s, but it was not displayed at that time. The plaque was stored until 1995, when volunteer firemen, with help from Mike Lesik, mounted and dedicated the plaque in front of the flagpole at the Occidental fire station. (Courtesy Barbara Gonnella.)

Nine

ARTS AND
ENTERTAINMENT

By 1898, there were six social clubs in Occidental. Social club members played cards, presented school recitals, sponsored dances, performed stage shows, and held meetings. These clubs also hosted picnics and barbecues. The Native Sons of the Golden West is a fraternal and patriotic organization that built a large social hall in Occidental in 1903 for these types of activities. The Order of the Druids was another, primarily Italian, social club, which separated the sexes similar to the socialization in small Italian towns. By the 1920s and 1930s, Occidental also had three pool halls, bocce courts, and several saloons.

Saloons have been an important part of Occidental since its inception. In November 1881, the *Petaluma Weekly Argus* reported that a small anti-alcohol temperance movement had been started in Occidental, stating that "One temperance organization has 2 members—one is a saloon keeper." Small local movements like this helped lead to Prohibition in 1920, when the production, transportation, and sale of all alcohol was banned. But Prohibition often seemed to target the poor, and there was corruption in its enforcement, so bootleggers near Occidental worked together to produce liquor and avoid Federal agents.

Both baseball and football were popular sports in Occidental by the turn of the 20th century. Football was played without modern padding, which increased the likelihood of injuries. An Occidental baseball team, jokingly called the "Fighting Irish" since the team was almost all Italian, was a local semiprofessional team in Sonoma County after World War II.

Since the 1970s, the Occidental area has attracted many artists, craftspeople, and world-class musicians—including Mickey Hart, Nick Gravenites, Tom Waites, and Les Claypool. Some artists and musicians were also attracted to the communes set up in the area in the 1970s, in particular Morningstar Ranch and Wheeler Ranch. Wheeler Ranch was started by Bill Wheeler, who was also a well-known painter of open spaces. Occidental has a rich history of supporting artists and musicians, leading to the acclaimed Occidental Center for the Arts and Redwood Arts Council.

ENTERTAINMENT IN 1900. Many social interactions were at the homes of friends and family, but by 1900, the number of activities at entertainment and social halls had greatly increased. They included shows, lectures, debates, dances, plays, and concerts. Men in town would also go to saloons to drink and play cards. This photograph shows the Native Sons Hall and Ciucci Saloon. (Courtesy Sonoma County Library.)

MARCHING BAND AT CHURCH, 1905. Marching bands originated on the battlefield, but are currently more associated with football games in America. The popularity and quality of marching bands increased after World War II. Performing outside St. Philip the Apostle Catholic Church is a marching band from San Francisco. (Courtesy Sonoma County Library.)

POPULAR MUSIC, 1911. A group of four musicians are pictured at the Rugani home. Before phonographs and electric amplification became common, live musicians performing at homes was a popular form of entertainment. These musicians are, from left to right, John W. Gonnella, Ralph Mazzotti, Erminia (Bittner) Bones, and Bob Bittner. (Courtesy Harold Lapham.)

LOCAL MUSICIANS, C. 1925. In 1909, Raffaello "Ralph" Mazzotti Sr. came from Italy, worked as a laborer, made Christmas wreaths, and collected mulch and leaf mold in the woods around Occidental. He is shown holding a guitar. Before World War II, the accordion was also a popular instrument in the area—it was portable, expressive, and loud. (Courtesy Harold Lapham.)

MUTT AND JEFF. In 1907, Harry "Bud" Fisher created the first daily comic strip in the *San Francisco Chronicle*, *Mr. A. Mutt*, about a racetrack gambler. In a 1908 comic, Mutt met his friend Jeff in an insane asylum. It is believed that Fisher got his idea for the character of Jeff when his train was stopped in Occidental. Fisher saw a four-foot, eight-inch hunchbacked man with a mustache, likely creamery owner "Jakie" Fehr, in an altercation with a lanky "candy butcher" from the train. The term "Mutt and Jeff" is still used in popular culture for a pair of individuals of mismatched sizes. (Wikimedia Commons.)

"HOLD UP," C. 1917. This humorous photograph was likely taken at the Union Hotel bar. Ralph Mazzotti is jokingly "holding up" Amerigo Gonnella. Amerigo was only 22 years old when he died, leaving a widow, daughter, and unborn son. Ralph Mazzotti Sr. also suffered a devastating loss when his son Ralph Mazzotti Jr. died after football practice at Tomales High School—he was only 16 years old. (Courtesy Frank and Barbara Gonnella family.)

EARLY FOOTBALL, C. 1898. The Occidental school building constructed in 1864 on Harrison Grade Road predates the town of Occidental—the town name was related to the preexisting school district name. Football gained popularity in the early 20th century, but it was a dangerous sport with minimal rules and minimal physical protection. This photograph shows players at the Occidental school. (Courtesy Sonoma County Library.)

THE "FIGHTING IRISH" BASEBALL TEAM, 1947. The Occidental team coached by Joe Gonnella finished in fourth place in the Sonoma County semiprofessional league in 1947. The team had a sense of humor—almost all of the members were Italian, except for Irish pitcher Charles Kelly. Other players included Lunardi, Pelletti, Panelli, Marra, Mazzotti, Montafi, two Panizzeras, two Fioris, and five Gonnellas. (Courtesy Frank and Barbara Gonnella family.)

ELECTRICITY, TELEPHONE, AND RADIO, C. 1924. The world was quickly changing in the early 20th century, especially due to the rapid expansion of electrical lines, telephone lines, and radio. In 1878, the *Petaluma Weekly Argus* said that Professor Alley gave an exhibition of electric lights in Occidental. William Borba, known as "Radio Bill," was a dealer in Sebastopol for Victor talking machines, radios, and Kodak cameras. This 1924 photograph shows some of his merchandise displayed at a Meeker District school. (Courtesy Sonoma County Library.)

HISTORIAN HAROLD LAPHAM, 1929. Harold Lapham was born on the Lapham Ranch on Marra Road in Occidental in 1924. His family has lived in Occidental since the mid-19th century. Lapham is a scholar and a local historian whose generosity with information and photographs greatly helped with this book. He is seen here at five years old, riding a cart pulled by a goat. (Courtesy Harold Lapham.)

ORR HALL, C. 1930. In 1906, Thomas Orr purchased the Native Sons Hall, which was then known as Orr Hall. The hall was eventually sold again and became Druid's Lodge. It was purchased by Tony and Clara Fiori in 1938, who owned it until it was destroyed by fire in 1951. The hall is the large building near left center. (Courtesy Harold Lapham.)

HANGING OUT, C. 1947. Young boys would hang out at the gas station in town or explore the nearby woods. It was an age when one had to make his or her own fun. From left to right are (first row) Benny Lunardi, Joe Negri Jr., "Skippy" Clark, Lawrin Mara, and (second row) Jerry Connell in back. (Courtesy Eleanor Travaglini.)

Morningstar and Other Communes, c. 1970. Morningstar Ranch was an open-land counterculture commune available to all. The ranch was in this form from 1967 to 1972. Cofounder Louis Gottlieb was fined and jailed for not forcing the people off the land. Gottlieb tried to leave his land to God, but the courts rejected this suggestion. California governor Ronald Reagan made it clear that he was no fan of Morningstar. This group photograph was taken at Star Mountain commune, adjacent to the Wheeler Ranch commune. (Courtesy Jessica Wheeler.)

Bill Wheeler with Daughter, Wheeler Ranch, 1971. Many of the young people eventually forced to move from Morningstar Ranch relocated to another nearby commune, Wheeler Ranch. The commune was simple, spontaneous, and off the grid, and clothing was optional. Wheeler promoted organic food, women's rights, environmental movements, and alternative medical and religious practices. Wheeler was also a well-known painter of open spaces. Bill Wheeler is pictured holding his daughter Jessica. (Courtesy Jessica Wheeler.)

WILLIE GONNELLA PLAYING THE ACCORDION, C. 1970. Willie Gonnella was a town character. He worked as a gardener, but also kept the town clean by pulling weeds and mowing vacant lots. He was best known for entertaining with his accordion, and he played at the Union Hotel bar for many years right up until his death in 1982. (Courtesy Frank and Barbara Gonnella family.)

NICK GRAVENITES. Nick Gravenites is a blues, rock, and folk singer, songwriter, and producer. He was the lead singer of Electric Flag and worked with Janis Joplin, Quicksilver Messenger Service, and Mike Bloomfield in the 1960s and 1970s. As a songwriter with the Paul Butterfield Blues Band, he was inducted into the Rock and Roll Hall of Fame in 2015. He still performs, including locally at the Union Hotel. He is seen here at left with bassist John Beckwith. (Courtesy Jack Journey.)

CARYL AND MICKEY HART. Caryl Hart is an environmental activist who started LandPaths (a land trust and trail advocacy organization), was director of Sonoma County Parks, and has been appointed to the state coastal commission. Mickey Hart is a percussionist and musicologist, best known for his work with the Grateful Dead, for which he was inducted into the Rock and Roll Hall of Fame. Both Mickey and Caryl said that everything good about their lives stems from choosing to live in Occidental. Mickey added, "There is an atmospheric power here . . . almost magical, surreal . . . smells, sounds, peaceful place to live." (Courtesy Barbara Gonnella.)

MUSIC TRADITION CONTINUES. Gien Gonnella, a fourth-generation Occidental Gonnella, can often be found playing piano for guests in the Bocce Ballroom of the Union Hotel. Her repertoire includes Beethoven, Tchaikovsky, and the Beatles. Gonnella also gives lessons to local budding pianists. She is a young bohemian artist, whose music adds to the local culture and continues the rich musical tradition of Occidental. (Courtesy Jack Journey.)

Ten

RETROSPECTIVE

After railroad service stopped in 1930 and the Great Depression began, there was an economic decline in Occidental and the population decreased. The primary attraction at that time was the Italian restaurants, and this remains true today. Some of the original Italian families are now gone; however, other pioneer Italian families have remained in the area and continue to be important members of the community. A partial list of these families includes the Panizzeras, Negris, Calvis, Gonnellas, Lunardis, and Mazzottis.

The townspeople are united in maintaining the charm and community of Occidental through historic preservation, selective development, support of music and the arts, and environmental sustainability. For example, the Occidental Center for the Arts attracts world-class talent in performing and visual arts. The Occidental Arts and Ecology Center is a research and advocacy center for biological and cultural diversity. Occidental is protected by the dedicated men and women of the volunteer fire department, and an annual picnic sponsored by the Occidental VFD always has community support.

Although Occidental is not an incorporated town, it has been able to maintain its character and beauty because of education, concern, and activism of the community. In 1875, American horticulturist Luther Burbank said that Sonoma County is "the chosen spot on earth as far as nature is concerned." The people who live in Occidental would undoubtedly agree, and perhaps jokingly suggest that Luther Burbank might have been more specific if he had waited another year until the town of Occidental had been named.

OCCIDENTAL ORIGINS, C. 1879. This is one of the oldest photographs of Occidental, a town that has frequently and abruptly changed throughout its early history, often because of fires. Some of the pioneer families have been more stable than this landscape, choosing to remain in the area with their neighbors, friends, and families. (Courtesy Harold Lapham.)

OCCIDENTAL EVOLUTION, C. 1970. Occidental, like much of the United States, underwent a period of stability and prosperity after the end of World War II. The town, still relatively isolated by location, continues to be a destination for scenic drives and authentic Italian food. This photograph shows the parking lot behind the Union Hotel on a busy day. (Courtesy Frank and Barbara Gonnella family.)

NATURAL PRESERVATION. The people near Occidental realize their ongoing responsibility to be good stewards of the land, especially protecting the redwood forests with their native plants and animals. A 33-acre grove of mature coastal redwoods near Fitzpatrick Lane remains, the only privately owned preserve in Sonoma County. Save the Redwoods League and LandPaths saved this area from logging in 2000. (Courtesy Mary Pozzi.)

HISTORIC PRESERVATION. The Occidental Historic District is a contiguous area consisting of approximately 103 properties. It includes many mid- to late-19th-century Greek Revival, Queen Anne, and Stick/Eastlake styles representative of a small, 19th-century rural community in Sonoma County. An example is the Taylor Building, shown here. It was constructed in 1886 and is now home to Howard's Station Café. (Courtesy Sonoma County Library.)

RESTAURANT RIVALRY, C. 1950. There have long been rumors of a rivalry among the Italian restaurants in town—once three—Fiori's, the Union Hotel, and Negri's, but now down to two. The October 2002 *San Francisco Magazine* says the Union Hotel and Negri's "have battled over everything from parking to who's the 'original.' " In reality, many members of both families have long been friends with each other. From left to right are three unidentified, Joe Negri Sr., Lucille Gonnella from the Union Hotel, and Joe Murphy. (Courtesy Frank and Barbara Gonnella family.)

EVOLUTION OF UNION HOTEL, C. 2007. Many changes have occurred at the Union Hotel. A new dining area was added in 1941, connecting the main building with the Bocce Ballroom. In 1958, the kitchen was enlarged, and in 1960, the nearby Union Motel was built. In 1984, an outdoor patio area was created; in 1990, a bakery/café was added; and in 1992, a pizzeria was opened. The Union Hotel is now run by Lucille and Mahoney Gonnella's son Frank and his wife, Barbara. (Courtesy Barbara Gonnella.)

EVOLUTION OF NEGRI'S. Negri's Restaurant was damaged by fire in 1969 and rebuilt. The bar has been recently remodeled and named Joe's Bar. The restaurant area sign reads, "Italian kitchen," emphasizing the authentic Italian food that Negri's has served for over 70 years. This is a recent photograph of Negri's. (Courtesy Barbara Gonnella.)

OCCIDENTAL AREA HEALTH CENTER. When Greg Rosa (pictured) was in medical school, he and his wife, Kathy, went for a drive and got stuck in a ravine near Occidental. After graduating, he learned that Occidental needed a doctor, and remembering the friendly and helpful people there, Rosa, with the help of local residents, formed the Occidental Area Health Clinic in 1976. (Courtesy Barbara Gonnella.)

OCCIDENTAL VOLUNTEER FIRE DEPARTMENT, 1971. After multiple devastating fires in the town's early history, a volunteer fire department was finally formed in 1945 with the backing of Mary Panizzera and local businesses. Joe Panizzera became the first fire chief. From left to right are Louie Gonnella, Domonic Travelini, Dario Montofi, and Joe Lunardi. (Courtesy Occidental Volunteer Fire Department.)

ANNUAL VFD BARBECUE. A fundraising barbecue was started in 1958 in conjunction with the Camp Meeker VFD. Admission was $1.25 for adults and 75¢ for children. According to the 1958 *Press Democrat*, the chicken barbecue also featured games, cakes, coffee, and beer. This is a more recent scene from this fundraising tradition. (Courtesy Occidental Volunteer Fire Department.)

LODGING IN OCCIDENTAL. Occidental has a long history of providing lodging for railroad families, loggers, and other guests. The Gonnella Occidental Guest House has three cottages in beautiful settings, and the Inn at Occidental is a romantic bed-and-breakfast. Pictured here is the Occidental Lodge, a friendly and convenient 1970s-style motor lodge owned by the Negri family. (Courtesy Barbara Gonnella.)

CAFÉS. Besides the two well-known Italian restaurants in town, there are a number of cafés that serve excellent food. Howard's Station Café, for example, is named after one of the founders of Occidental and is located in the historic Taylor Building. The menu includes healthy and organic foods, including a popular breakfast and lunch menu. The café is owned and operated by Chris and Terry Martin. (Courtesy Barbara Gonnella.)

FINE ART AND CRAFTS. Since the early 1970s, Occidental has attracted artists and artisans. Hand Goods, for example, was established in Occidental in 1970 to showcase local artists' work. Artist Nancy Farah created and ran Hand Goods for 25 years, but it has transitioned to longtime employee Heidi Schmidt. The store includes work from the finest potters, painters, textile makers, and jewelers. (Courtesy Barbara Gonnella.)

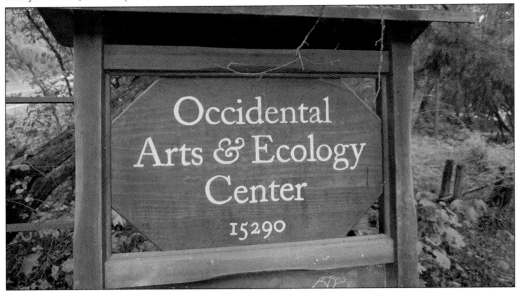

OCCIDENTAL ARTS AND ECOLOGY CENTER. Founded in 1994, the OAEC is a research, demonstration, education, advocacy, and community-organizing center that develops strategies for resilience and restoration of biological and cultural diversity. Projects include organic gardens, preservation of grasslands and local forests, and intentional communities. The intentional communities movement's purpose is to weave together family, work, home, social change, spirituality, celebration, and friends. (Courtesy Barbara Gonnella.)

OCCIDENTAL CENTER FOR THE ARTS AND REDWOOD ARTS COUNCIL. In 1998, Occidental activist Doris Murphy and Redwood Arts Council founder Kit Neustadter founded the Occidental Center for the Arts (OCA), a nonprofit that provides high-quality arts and cultural events to the area. The OCA supports diverse cultural experiences, performances, visual art education and exhibitions, and literary events. The Redwood Arts Council, which hosts a world-class chamber music series, and Occidental Community Choir have moved their homes to the OCA. (Courtesy Barbara Gonnella.)

COMMUNITY TRADITIONS, HOLIDAY CAROLING. Each December, friends and families in Sonoma County drive through the redwoods to sing Christmas carols at the Occidental Union Hotel. The Bocce Ballroom is adorned with garlands, and freshly baked handcrafted cookies and hot spiced cider welcome the carolers. Traditions like these have brought the Occidental community together for over 140 years. (Courtesy Barbara Gonnella.)

BIBLIOGRAPHY

Chapman, Tom. *Norma's Memory Book*. Occidental, CA: Self-published, 1993.

————. *One Man's Family*. Occidental, CA: Self-published, 1995.

Charles, George. *Memories of the Sonoma Coast*. Santa Rosa, CA: Legacy Press, 1996.

Dickinson, A. Bray. *Narrow Gauge to the Redwoods: The Story of the North Pacific Coast-Railroad and San Francisco Bay Paddle Wheel Ferries*. Los Angeles, CA: Trans-Anglo Books, 1970.

Hill, Amie. *An Historical and Anecdotal Walking Tour of the Small (but Fascinating) Village of Occidental, California*. Occidental, CA: self-published, 1997.

Nevins, Don. *Of Towers and Trees and Towering Men*. South Hackensack, NJ: Ecclesiastical Color Publishers, 1969.

Stindt, Fred A. *Trains to the Russian River*. Kelseyville, CA: self-published, 1974.

Torliatt, Lee. *Golden Memories of the Redwood Empire*. Charleston, SC: Arcadia Publishing, 2001.

Vecoli, Rudolph J. *Italian Immigrants in Rural and Small Town America*. New York, NY: American Italian Historical Association, 1987.

INDEX

Discover Thousands of Local History Books
Featuring Millions of Vintage Images

Arcadia Publishing, the leading local history publisher in the United States, is committed to making history accessible and meaningful through publishing books that celebrate and preserve the heritage of America's people and places.

Find more books like this at
www.arcadiapublishing.com

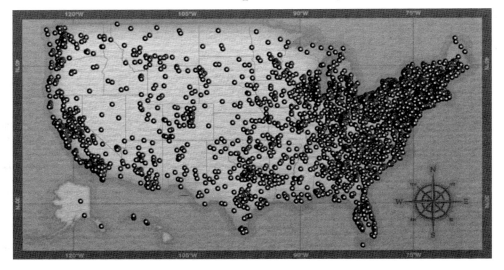

Search for your hometown history, your old stomping grounds, and even your favorite sports team.